H.L.—1

THE HAMLYN LECTURES

TWENTY-FIRST SERIES

THE BRITISH TRADITION IN CANADIAN LAW

AUSTRALIA
The Law Book Company Ltd.
Sydney : Melbourne : Brisbane

CANADA AND U.S.A.
The Carswell Company Ltd.
Toronto

INDIA
N. M. Tripathi Private Ltd.
Bombay

ISRAEL
Steimatzky's Agency Ltd.
Jerusalem : Tel Aviv : Haifa

NEW ZEALAND
Sweet & Maxwell (N.Z.) Ltd.
Wellington

PAKISTAN
Pakistan Law House
Karachi

THE BRITISH TRADITION IN CANADIAN LAW

BY

The Honourable
BORA LASKIN, LL.D., D.C.L., F.R.S.C.
A Member of the Court of Appeal of Ontario

Published under the auspices of
THE HAMLYN TRUST

LONDON
STEVENS & SONS
1969

Published in 1969 by
Stevens & Sons Limited of
11 New Fetter Lane in the
City of London and printed
in Great Britain by The
Eastern Press Ltd. of London
and Reading.

SBN 420 42880 1/91

CONTENTS

THE HAMLYN LECTURES

1949 Freedom under the Law
by The Rt. Hon. Lord Denning

1950 The Inheritance of the Common Law
by Richard O'Sullivan, Esq.

1951 The Rational Strength of English Law
by Professor F. H. Lawson

1952 English Law and the Moral Law
by Dr. A. L. Goodhart

1953 The Queen's Peace
by Sir Carleton Kemp Allen

1954 Executive Discretion and Judicial Control
by Professor C. J. Hamson

1955 The Proof of Guilt
by Dr. Glanville Williams

1956 Trial by Jury
by The Rt. Hon. Lord Devlin

1957 Protection from Power under English Law
by The Rt. Hon. Lord MacDermott

1958 The Sanctity of Contracts in English Law
by Sir David Hughes Parry

1959 Judge and Jurist in the Reign of Victoria
by C. H. S. Fifoot, Esq.

1960 The Common Law in India
by M. C. Setalvad, Esq.

1961 British Justice: The Scottish Contribution
by Professor T. B. Smith

THE HAMLYN TRUST

THE Hamlyn Trust came into existence under the will of the late Miss Emma Warburton Hamlyn, of Torquay, who died in 1941, at the age of eighty. She came of an old and well-known Devon family. Her father, William Bussell Hamlyn, practised in Torquay as a solicitor for many years. She was a woman of strong character, intelligent and cultured, well versed in literature, music and art, and a lover of her country. She inherited a taste for law, and studied the subject. She also travelled frequently on the Continent and about the Mediterranean, and gathered impressions of comparative jurisprudence and ethnology.

Miss Hamlyn bequeathed the residue of her estate in terms which were thought vague. The matter was taken to the Chancery Division of the High Court, which on November 29, 1948, approved a Scheme for the administration of the Trust. Paragraph 3 of the Scheme is as follows:—

> "The object of the charity is the furtherance by lectures or otherwise among the Common People of the United Kingdom of Great Britain and Northern Ireland of the knowledge of the Comparative Jurisprudence and the Ethnology of the chief European countries including the United Kingdom, and the circumstances of the growth of such jurisprudence to the intent that the Common People of the United Kingdom may realise the privileges which in law and custom they enjoy in comparison with other European Peoples and realising and appreciating such privileges may recognise the responsibilities and obligations attaching to them."

From the first the Trustees decided to organise courses of lectures of outstanding interest and quality by persons of eminence, under the auspices of co-operating universities or other bodies, with a view to the lectures being made available in book form to a wide public.

The Twenty-first Series of Hamlyn Lectures was delivered in December, 1969, by the Honourable Bora Laskin in the Inner Temple.

J. N. D. ANDERSON,
Chairman of the Trustees.

November, 1969.

To

PEGGY

PREFACE

THE hospitable terms of the Hamlyn Trust easily contain my subject "The British Tradition in Canadian Law." However misleading it might be thought to use the word "British" instead of "English"—one looks in vain for any strictly Scottish influence on Canadian law—I have felt justified in using the broader term, notwithstanding the fact that it is English law and English legal institutions with which I am concerned in these lectures. The British Monarch, the British Cabinet, the British Parliament and such British courts as the House of Lords and the Judicial Committee of the Privy Council (I cannot characterise it as other than British despite its overseas members), have played major roles in the establishment of Canadian legal institutions and in the directions taken by Canadian law. A qualification must be entered with respect to the distinctive civil law system of Quebec; but even there the judicial apparatus is English rather than French-inspired, and Canadian federalism has brought a further English dimension to both legislation and adjudication affecting that Province.

What a Toronto correspondent wrote in 1856 in a letter to the *Law Times* (28 L.T. 85) about England and Upper Canada has a familiar ring even today in respect of England and common law Canada; he said:

> "The laws of the two countries are almost identical. The practice or administration of the law is the same in each country. . . . I do not invite an emigration of English lawyers, for in Upper Canada the profession is well supplied from native sources. But it will be a

> consolation to such members of the English Bar as may resolve to enter into competition in the colonies to know that they will labour under no disadvantage."

One such member felt that his English bar qualification entitled him to offer this competition without satisfying the requirements of the Law Society of Upper Canada; and he even fought for this view in the courts, but without success: see *Re de Sousa* (1885) 9 O.R. 39.

The similarities spoken of above were not, of course, coincidental but were originally coerced; and later, as to all of Canada save Quebec, they came to represent a tradition under whose influence Canadian courts were content to dwell and in whose source they seemed to find most if not all of the inspiration that they required for the discharge of their duties. This dependence long ago ceased to be either necessary or admirable. Its persistence is a tribute not alone to the strength of habit, but as well to the vigour of the tradition in the hands of its expositors in the United Kingdom.

It is a signal feature of the Hamlyn Trust lectures that they are published contemporaneously with oral delivery; and such relief as the lecturer has in having previously handed over a final manuscript must be tempered by the fear that errors that might have been caught during or after formal presentation of the lectures are beyond recall or remedy. I say this here because I tapped many sources in preparing these lectures, but have not identified all of them lest I overrun the text with an extravagance of footnotes; and hence, the responsibility for mistakes or for exhibited ignorance is all the more mine.

I thank the Trustees of the Hamlyn Trust for the honour

of the invitation to be a Hamlyn Trust lecturer; I join a distinguished company.

My secretary, Miss Ann Brumell, typed my manuscript through many hot summer days and I express my appreciation for her cheerful assistance.

The dedication to my wife is a small recognition of an unredeemable debt.

BORA LASKIN.

1

RECEPTION: THE COURTS AND THE PROFESSION

MORE than two hundred years have passed since English law and English legal institutions were rooted in a yet unborn Canada. Sustained at first by remote control from Westminster and by domestic control of colonial governors, the English tradition has survived Canadian legislative and judicial independence, and remains a vital and omnipresent force in Canadian law. I speak of the English tradition deliberately rather than the common law tradition, because it is the English common law and not its sturdy varieties in the United States, or even in Australia and New Zealand, that continues to have a dominant influence in Canadian courts. The British Parliament no longer provides the steady stream of prototypes for the Canadian Statute Book that was evident in the 19th century and in the early part of the 20th; but British courts, the House of Lords and the Judicial Committee of the Privy Council, and even the English Court of Appeal, are still a habitual resort for Canadian judges at all levels of the judicial establishment.

The existence of a civil law system in a part of the Canadian heartland has had hardly any mitigating effect upon the persistence in other parts of Canada of the English common law example. Indeed, such reciprocal influences as have been evident testify to a more pronounced effect of the common law upon the civil law system than the reverse. Nor has Canadian political federalism resulted in any substantial modification of the application of the English common law. Because of the long-time judicial ascendancy of the Privy Council in delimiting the respective spheres of central and provincial legislative authority, British statutory models and English common law conceptions, fashioned and nourished in a unitary state, have played an important role in fixing the content as well as the division of the categories of law-making power in Canada. They have been particularly significant for Quebec in those areas of private law which after 1867 were withdrawn from provincial competence and reposed in the central Parliament, as, for example, negotiable instruments, and bankruptcy and insolvency.

It is not, however, the total tradition that either was introduced or has survived. The introduction of English law in the 18th and 19th centuries into the then separate constituents of a later Canada, whether on the principle of colonies by conquest (as in the case of Quebec) or on the half-truth of colonies by settlement (as in the case of the Atlantic Provinces) had to take account of the rude realities of small settlements, with hardly any resources of professional manpower and beset by difficulties of communication. It would have been odd, for example, to bring to these undeveloped lands the Order of the Coif, or to expect the communities to accept the barrister-solicitor or barrister-attorney distinction which at the time was recognised in England. Not that there were no attempts in the latter direction. When the Law Society of Upper Canada was established in 1797, a proposal was made to adopt this English practice. It was rejected, as were similar proposals made at intervals to the end of the first half of the 19th century.[1] Nonetheless, other English legal institutions and

[1] See Riddell, *The Legal Profession in Upper Canada* (1916) at pp. 16–19; *cf.* Sedgwick, "Unfusing the Profession" (1955) 33 Can. Bar Rev. 499.

principles, equally not in keeping with the pioneer societies of the colonies, were fastened upon them as being in the nature of their heritage.

Reception

There are various " in force " dates of the reception of English law in the various common law Provinces and in the territories of Canada. Their effect was simply to fix the time as of which then existing British legislation and English judge-made law became, so far as applicable or so far as by reason of local circumstances they were not inapplicable, part of the law of the particular colony. This pre-packaged body of law could be changed, of course, by local legislation, subject to the superior dictate of the British Parliament, a dictate which came to an end formally with the Statute of Westminster 1931. Again, it could be modified by local judicial decision. But, more important, the dates of reception, so far as the English common law was concerned, moved forward both through a habit of assimilation and also under the compulsion of *stare decisis* by reason of the governing effect of Privy Council determinations and, through it, of the decisions of the House of Lords under the principle of *Robins* v. *National Trust Co.*[2] The decisions of these tribunals ceased to be formally binding with the abolition of Privy Council appeals in 1949, but their influence since that date has remained stronger than any other in the judicial business of Canada, saving, of course, the authority of the Supreme Court of Canada.

Quebec, as the post-1763 Canada for almost three decades, also had its " in force " date for English law, but the

[2] [1927] A.C. 515.

extent of its application remained unclear for a decade. No doubt the military conquest changed the public law, at least in those incidents pertaining to the new relation of the inhabitants as subjects of the British King.[3] The Royal Proclamation of October 7, 1763, reiterating in part the Articles of Capitulation of 1760, which guaranteed to the inhabitants the enjoyment of their property and freedom of worship, assured them of freedom of worship "so far as the laws of Great Britain permit." It promised them an assembly but left to the discretion of the Governor, under his instructions, the timing of its establishment; and pending elections to and summoning of the assembly, the populace was to have "the enjoyment of the benefit of the laws of our realm of England." [4]

Scholars of the period have debated, with the help of hindsight provided by *Campbell* v. *Hall*, decided in 1774,[5] whether the Proclamation swept away the whole of the French law which had prevailed in the country. Governor Murray's Ordinance of September 17, 1764, established a judicial system in some imitation of the English, and the judges of the civil Court of Common Pleas were enjoined thereby "to determine agreeable to equity, having regard nevertheless to the laws of England as far as the circumstances and present situation of things will permit." The reference to "equity" and to the circumscription of English law by local circumstances resulted in the continued

[3] This is still a live issue in present-day Canadian federalism, reflected in *Saumur* v. *City of Quebec* [1953] 2 S.C.R. 299, touching the distribution of law-making power in the matter of the political civil liberties, *e.g.*, freedom of speech and of religion.

[4] See the narrative in Neatby, *Quebec* (*The Revolutionary Age 1760–1791*) (1966), pp. 15–16, p. 45 *et seq.*

[5] (1774) 1 Cowp. 204; 98 E.R. 1045.

application of the French civil law in disputes among the French-speaking Canadians; but there was confusion which continued until the Quebec Act of 1774 resolved the matter by affirming that in all matters of controversy relative to property and civil rights resort was to be had to the laws of Canada, that is to the French law that had been in force in the country. The same Act provided, however, that "the criminal law of England . . . shall continue to be administered, and shall be observed as law in the Province of Quebec." The uniform observance of the English criminal law in British North America was carried into the confederation scheme in 1867 when, unlike the position in the United States and in Australia, exclusive jurisdiction was conferred upon the central Parliament in relation to criminal law and criminal procedure.

With the separation of English-speaking Upper Canada from Quebec (Lower Canada), effected by an order-in-council under the Constitutional Act 1791, the first statute enacted by the new legislature of Upper Canada swept away the French law and introduced the English civil law as of October 15, 1792, and provided also for the introduction of the English rules of evidence "in the several Courts of law and equity in this Province." The last-mentioned reference to equity was a barren exercise because Upper Canada had no Court of Chancery until 1837. In 1800, Upper Canada formally adopted the English criminal law as of September 17, 1792.

The reception of English law in the other Provinces stood as follows.[6] Nova Scotia, then embracing what later (1784)

[6] See Falconbridge, *Banking and Bills of Exchange* (6th ed., 1956), pp. 11–14; and Cote, "The Introduction of English Law into Alberta" (1964) 3 Alta.L.Rev. 262.

was separated as New Brunswick, and Newfoundland may be said to have received the corpus of English law (including the statute law), so far as applicable, as it stood immediately before October 3, 1758, and January 1, 1833, being the dates, respectively, of the meetings of the first legislative assemblies of those colonies. The principle was expressed by a Newfoundland court in 1822, namely, that "colonial courts date the discontinuance of English statute laws, not from the time of the colony being settled, but from the institution of a local legislature in the colony."[7] Prince Edward Island, known as St. John's Island until 1798 when it became (for the second time) a separate colony after having been previously first annexed to and later associated with Nova Scotia, became subject to the laws of England under the Royal Proclamation of October 7, 1763, following the Treaty of Paris.

British Columbia, by local statute, introduced the law of England as of November 19, 1858, so far as it was not by reason of local circumstances inapplicable. The date is important for its embrace of the Matrimonial Causes Act 1857. Disagreement among British Columbia judges as to the force of this statute in British Columbia was resolved by the Privy Council in 1908 in favour of its domestic application.[8] Other Provinces which had earlier "in force" dates for English law, for example, Nova Scotia and Ontario, adopted the enactment or parts of it by express legislation.

The "in force" dates for English law in the three

[7] *Young* (*Yonge*) v. *Blaikie* (1822) 1 Nfld.L.R. 277 at p. 283.
[8] *Watt* v. *Watt* [1908] A.C. 573.

prairie Provinces have a special history.[9] It begins with the charter of May 2, 1670, to the Hudson's Bay Company which was endowed thereunder with legislative and judicial power in the vast western territory of Rupert's Land, such power to be exercised by the Governor and Council in conformity with the law, statutes and customs of England. This was a dormant jurisdiction for almost a century and a half. Moreover, on the judicial side, trials of white persons committing serious offences in the territory had to take place in England. In 1803, alleviation of the enormous waste of time and money that this entailed was sought by conferring criminal jurisdiction upon the courts of Lower Canada or, if the Governor thereof certified to greater convenience, upon the courts of Upper Canada. This scheme applied, in the words of the statute, to the "Indian Territories" which were thought to include Rupert's Land, and the Canadian courts acted upon this view. Doubts upon the question, emphasised by counsel's opinion given by Sir Samuel Romilly, were resolved by an Imperial Statute of 1821 whereby concurrent civil and criminal jurisdiction over the territory of the Hudson's Bay Company was vested in the courts of Upper and Lower Canada. This in turn tended to dry up as developing settlements in the area saw the emergence of a local judiciary.

Following provision in 1867 and 1868 for surrender of the Hudson's Bay Company lands to the Crown and for the acquisition of these and other portions of the north-western territory by Canada—which was done—the Province of Manitoba was created in 1870 out of part of that area.

[9] See Colwyn Williams, "The Dawn of Law on the Prairies" (1962) 27 Sask. Bar Rev. 126; (1963) 28 Sask. Bar Rev. 17, 63.

Since this was post-confederation, any adoption of a reception statute had to take account of the distribution of legislative power. Thus it was that both Manitoba, in 1874, and Canada, in 1888, enacted legislation fixing July 15, 1870, as the reception date of English law in the Province.

Sinclair v. *Mulligan* illustrates the peculiar situation in which Manitoba found itself before the foregoing reception statutes were introduced.[10] The Statute of Frauds 1677 would not have been part of its law when it received only English statute law as of May 2, 1670; nor would matters within federal jurisdiction have been introduced by the provincial statute of 1874. Alberta and Saskatchewan were not beset by such difficulties. They were carved out of the North-West Territories in 1905 but prior to that time that region, being wholly under federal jurisdiction, was endowed by federal enactment in 1886 with the civil and criminal laws of England, also as of July 15, 1870, so far as applicable to the Territories. This prescription was included in the constituent Acts of the new Provinces in 1905.

The only present fascination of the reception principles and statutes is to comb the cases for exotic illustrations of absorption of English or United Kingdom statutes. There are many to be picked at random; for example, the Statute of Tenures 1660, which the Supreme Court of Canada (but not the Privy Council) treated as operable in Rupert's Land[11]; the Herbalists Act 1542, held to be in force in British Columbia whose existence was unknown at that

[10] (1888) 5 Man.R. 17.

[11] *Att.-Gen. Alta.* v. *Huggard Assets Ltd.* [1953] A.C. 420; reversing [1951] S.C.R. 427.

time [12]; and the Statute of Staples 1353, held to be in force in Nova Scotia.[13] I need not multiply examples. For present purposes, it is enough to note that there have been attempts at collection and listing of English and United Kingdom statutes which have been given force in Canadian Provinces or have been rejected as unsuitable.[14] To attempt such an exercise other than through the case law would involve painstaking research with uncertain results.

There is perhaps a more general problem of assessing suitability of both common law and legislation to local conditions, in terms of the relevant time as of which such assessment should be made. Clearly, this involves the double-barrelled exercise of examining suitability as of the time the issue arose in the provincial court, and considering whether at that time the reasons which prompted the adoption of the English rule or statute were still valid and relevant to the local situation. It is an easier exercise where statute rather than common law is concerned, because in the latter case the temptation to slip into *stare decisis* harness may be well-nigh irresistible.

In theory, a British statute, which is within the reception period, could be adopted or applied notwithstanding its subsequent repeal in Great Britain, known at the time the matter arose in the provincial court; similarly, with respect to a common law rule later abolished by British statute. In *Re Simpson*, which came before the Alberta courts in 1927, the rule in *Shelley's Case* was held to be inapplicable

12 *R.* v. *De Banou* (1968) 2 D.L.R. (3d) 424.

13 *The Dart* (1812) Stewart 301 at p. 307 (Nova Scotia Court of Vice-Admiralty).

14 See Clement, *The Canadian Constitution* (1916), p. 1060; Cote, "Table of English Statutes in Force in Canada" (1964) 3 Alta.L.Rev. 278; Roberts-Wray, *Commonwealth and Colonial Law* (1964), p. 549 *et seq.*

in that Province, but the fact of its abolition under the Law of Property Act 1925 was not a recorded consideration for that conclusion [15]; and the rule has been applied as fixed law in Ontario in a number of post-1925 decisions without reconsideration of its suitability.[16]

The Courts

England, in the 18th century, when the story of Canadian courts begins, had its Court of King's Bench, its Court of Common Pleas, its Court of Exchequer, with a " tangle of jurisdictions " (to use Plucknett's phrase) [17] on the common law side, and its Court of Chancery and the Court of Exchequer as well, on the equity side. Justices of the peace functioned in various ways at an inferior level. Neither in Nova Scotia nor in Quebec in that century—and it is in those areas that the Canadian judicial system took its rise—was such a distribution of jurisdiction either applicable or possible. A distinction could be understood between civil and criminal matters, but even then there could be no great indulgence in the luxury of separate courts.

Indeed, when civil government was established in Nova Scotia in 1749, the Governor and Council assumed judicial authority (in addition to legislative and executive) as a general court of original civil and criminal jurisdiction, embracing on its civil side both common law and equity. It also purported in its short career as such a court (it was

[15] [1927] 4 D.L.R. 817, affirmed without passing on the point, [1928] S.C.R. 329.

[16] See, for example, *Re Gracey* (1932) 41 O.W.N. 1 (hope expressed for Ontario legislation to abolish the rule); *Re Armstrong* [1943] O.W.N. 43.

[17] *Concise History of the Common Law* (5th ed., 1956), p. 210.

superseded by a Supreme Court in 1754) to exercise divorce jurisdiction.[18] This also occurred in New Brunswick where the Governor and Council, pursuant to statute, acted as a court of judicature in matrimonial causes for well over half a century until a new court of record in such matters was established in 1860.[19] In Prince Edward Island too the Governor and Council were constituted as a court of divorce in 1835. It was dormant, however, from Confederation until 1946, but its resumption of activity was cut short by legislation in 1949 which vested concurrent jurisdiction in the Supreme Court of the Province, with power of supersession.[20] The obvious comment is that in the three maritime Provinces divorce jurisdiction was a judicial matter at a time when in England it was legislative only.

To complete the narrative on divorce jurisdiction in Canada, it remained legislative for Ontario domiciliaries as well until 1930 [21] (although Ontario courts did have alimony jurisdiction), and also for those of Quebec and Newfoundland, until their courts joined in the administration of the new federal Divorce Act of 1968.[22] In all the Provinces west of Ontario the reception statutes embraced the English divorce and matrimonial causes legislation of 1857; and the Privy Council in a series of decisions affirmed the jurisdiction of their courts to entertain divorce petitions.[23]

The problems of court structure, jurisdiction and pro-

[18] See Townshend, " Historical Account of the Courts of Judicature in Nova Scotia " (1899) 19 C.L.T. 25, 58, 87, 142.

[19] See the historical account in *McLennan* v. *McLennan* [1939] 2 D.L.R. 622, affirmed [1940] S.C.R. 335.

[20] See *Reference re Divorce Act (P.E.I.)* [1952] 2 D.L.R. 513.

[21] See Divorce Act (Ontario) 1930 (Can.), c. 14.

[22] 1967–68 (Can.), c. 24.

[23] See *Walker* v. *Walker* [1919] A.C. 947; *Board* v. *Board* [1919] A.C. 956.

cedure for the four western Provinces were relatively simple compared to those faced by the older provinces. By the time of their establishment the reform movement in judicial organisation and procedures was well advanced in England, and they were immediate beneficiaries. There were never any separate courts of common law and of chancery in the four western Provinces; their Supreme Courts had no such problem as, for example, did the Supreme Court of New Brunswick in 1842 when it decided that it had no equity jurisdiction on its exchequer side but only common law jurisdiction.[24] In a word, the superior courts of the four western Provinces began with many of the benefits of the Judicature Acts, principally that of being able to administer law and equity in the same forum.

By contrast, the force of the English pattern in the latter half of the 18th century resulted in a separate administration of common law and equity in the maritime Provinces. The unified administration of justice, which began in Nova Scotia under the Governor and Council, supported by an inferior county court, and under procedures adopted from Virginia, broke down when the Supreme Court supplanted the Governor and Council on the common law side and left the Governor and Council with chancery jurisdiction until a Master of the Rolls was appointed in late 1825. The Governor as Chancellor retained appellate functions; and, as was common with respect to all superior court jurisdiction, there was a further appeal to the Privy Council. This separate equity jurisdiction was terminated in 1856 and vested in the Supreme Court, but a few years later an equity division was established in the Supreme Court with a judge

24 *Att.-Gen.* v. *Baillie* (1842) 3 N.B.R. 443.

separately assigned to it; and final fusion did not come until 1884.[25]

New Brunswick and Prince Edward Island exhibit a comparable history, save that in the case of the latter a separate chancery court survives to this day. In both Provinces the Governor exercised personally, or by delegation to the Chief Justice of the Supreme Court, the functions of a Chancellor. A Master of the Rolls took over the original jurisdiction in New Brunswick from 1838 and until the office and the separate administration of equity were terminated in 1854 and equity power was vested in the Supreme Court. In Prince Edward Island, a Master of the Rolls was appointed in 1848, and in 1869 a Vice-Chancellor, each being also appointed at the time assistant judges of the Supreme Court. This dual capacity still obtains, and those invested with it (being now full judges of the Supreme Court as well as Master of the Rolls and Vice-Chancellor respectively) exercise their different common law and equity powers in different courts and under the different procedures pertaining to those courts. There has, however, been some fusion, because the Supreme Court may give equitable relief in respect of claims otherwise properly brought in that court.[26]

Newfoundland has had a special judicial history, although its Supreme Court has had, from its founding, criminal and civil jurisdiction, including equitable jurisdiction. King William's Act of 1699 provided that all felonies committed in the island were triable in any county in

25 Townshend, " History of the Court of Chancery in Nova Scotia " (1900) 20 C.L.T. 14, 37, 74, 105.

26 See *Solomon* v. *Currie* (1965) 51 M.P.R. 252. The Rolls Court and the Vice-Chancellor's Court are continued under the Chancery Act, R.S. P.E.I. 1951, c. 21, as amended.

England under commissions of oyer and terminer and general gaol delivery. Criminal jurisdiction was not turned over to the local administration until 1750 when it was included in the Governor's commission. A court of Common Pleas was established by the Governor in 1790, but the next year British legislation provided for a court of civil jurisdiction for a one-year period. In 1793, a Supreme Court of Judicature, with criminal and civil jurisdiction was established, but with uncertain prospects of survival. More permanent arrangements were prescribed by British legislation of 1809; and finally in 1824 provision was made for establishment by royal charter of the Supreme Court of Newfoundland with comprehensive criminal and civil jurisdiction, and it began to function under this authority in 1826.[27]

In conquered Quebec, the judicial system established by Governor Murray's ordinance of September 17, 1764, provided for justices of the peace to entertain minor civil and criminal causes; for a Court of King's Bench with civil and criminal jurisdiction on a higher level; and for a Court of Common Pleas for civil causes only and to which the French-speaking Canadians were expected to resort. French-speaking advocates had right of audience in it, and the legal disabilities of Roman Catholics then still obtaining in the United Kingdom, were not applied to preclude them from sitting on juries in this court. Moreover, the ambiguous nature of the ordinance in its reference to the court ("the judges . . . are to determine agreeable to equity, having regard nevertheless to the laws of England . . .") resulted

[27] 1824 (U.K.), 5 Geo. 4, c. 67; and for the earlier statutes, see 1793 (U.K.), 33 Geo. 3, c. 46, and 1809 (U.K.), 49 Geo. 3, c. 27.

in the frequent application of French civil law. In 1770 the Court of Common Pleas succeeded to the civil jurisdiction of the justice of the peace (cases with an upper monetary limit of ten pounds) because the courts of those justices had proved unsatisfactory in terms of competence, time and expense.

The Quebec Act 1774, which restored French civil law but preserved the English criminal law, provided for the creation of a new system of judicature in place of the existing one. The American revolution intervened and, for a time, there were no courts functioning. The old system ended as of May 1, 1775, and the magistrates then appointed to administer justice had a short tenure. Ordinances in 1777 created a Court of Common Pleas for each of the districts of Quebec and Montreal (into which the colony was divided for this purpose) to exercise comprehensive civil jurisdiction only, with a limited right of appeal to the Governor and Council, and established a Court of King's Bench for the whole country with criminal jurisdiction only. For petty offences, a Court of General Sessions of the Peace was established separately for each of the two districts of Quebec and Montreal, to be presided over by Commissioners of the Peace.

A further ordinance in 1787 authorised the creation of new districts, and in pursuance of this power five new districts, each with its Court of Common Pleas, were established in 1788. Four of these were in territory which a few years later became the Province of Upper Canada.

The Constitutional Act 1791, under which Quebec was divided into Lower Canada and Upper Canada, protected existing administrative and judicial arrangements until changed by the appropriate authority. It added to them, however, by providing that the Governor in each Province and the Executive Council should be a Court of Appeal in civil matters as had previously been the case for the entire area under the Ordinance of 1777. In 1793 Lower Canada was divided into the three judicial districts of Quebec, Montreal and Three Rivers. A Court of King's Bench, with criminal and civil jurisdiction (in the latter case, reaching back to the pre-1759 French law), was established for both Quebec and Montreal, and it served Three Rivers as well, along with a summary small debt court. The following year the provincial Court of Appeal was reconstituted to include the Chief Justice of the Province (Quebec district) and the Chief Justice of the Montreal district with the Governor and the Executive Council, from which group a quorum of five could sit in civil appeals.

These judicial arrangements were radically altered in 1849 after intermediate changes which included the establishment of district courts and their subsequent abolition; the establishment of circuit courts; and the creation of a new Court of Appeal for Lower Canada, consisting of all the judges of the Courts of Queen's Bench, and with jurisdiction in civil matters. Two measures in 1849 gave form to a new scheme of judicature which is, in substance, still in force.[28] A Court of Queen's Bench was established as a court of record with appellate jurisdiction in civil matters and with original criminal jurisdiction. The existing Courts of Queen's Bench were abolished, and a Superior Court with broad civil jurisdiction was created. In the result, Quebec alone of

[28] 1849 (Can.), cc. 37 and 38.

the Provinces does not have county or district courts of the kind that exist elsewhere in Canada, although it does have inferior courts with small claim and penal jurisdiction.

At the present time the Quebec Court of Queen's Bench exercises appellate jurisdiction in civil and criminal matters and original criminal jurisdiction; and the Superior Court, whose judges exercise their functions in assigned districts, is in the main a court of civil jurisdiction but has appellate criminal jurisdiction in summary conviction matters.[29]

The statutory continuity of the law and of the judicial system of undivided Quebec into the new colony of Upper Canada under the Constitutional Act 1791 was a mere holding provision pending expected changes. The introduction of English law on the civil side, along with trial by jury, in 1792 was followed by a Judicature Act in 1794 which brought in familiar elements of the English system. The Court of Common Pleas, which had operated on a district system before the separation of Upper Canada, was dissolved and a centralised Court of King's Bench was established, with civil and criminal jurisdiction. Associated with it were characteristic provisions for assizes and trials at *nisi prius*, and for commissions of oyer and terminer and general gaol delivery. The whole worked out that both civil and criminal cases could be heard at the same assizes.

The imposition of a complex English judicial structure and procedure upon a sparsely inhabited and undeveloped colony evoked some critical comment, equally apt for other Canadian areas to which it was applied [30]:

[29] Courts of Justice Act, R.S.Q. 1964, c. 20, as amended.

[30] *Simcoe Papers*, Vol. 2, p. 270, by Richard Cartwright, a leading merchant who became a Common Pleas judge in 1788 and a member of the Legislative Council of Upper Canada in 1792.

> "For see it comes with all the glorious uncertainties of the law in its train, holding out wealth and distinction to the man of law but poverty and distress to the unfortunate client . . . it comes with all its hydra of demurrers, rejoinders, surrejoinders, rebutters and surrebutters, and all the monstrous offspring of metaphysical subtlety begotten upon chicane, to swallow up our simple forms and modes of process which are easy to be understood and followed by any man of plain sense and common education."

More serious for Upper Canada than a complex procedure whose reform was a half century in the future, was the want of a court of equity. Unlike the case in the maritime Provinces, where the prerogative view of the Governor's office included a function as Chancellor, this did not take hold in Upper Canada. The Court of King's Bench was a common law court only, from which an appeal lay to the Governor or the Chief Justice and any two members of the Council as a Court of Appeal and thence to the Privy Council. Although district or division Courts of Requests presided over by justices of the peace were provided for under an Upper Canada Act of 1792, they were, even though somewhat like poor men's courts of conscience on the English example, merely small debt courts and did not answer the need for a court of equity.

The need of a court with equitable jurisdiction was recognised in the intermittent efforts made over three decades to secure one. As the late Dean Falconbridge put it, "there was no jurisdiction to enforce trusts, to grant injunctions, to decree specific performance, to compel discovery or to give relief against legal proceedings prosecuted contrary to equity and good conscience nor any machinery to take accounts or to supervise the administration of estates."[31] The most telling illustration of the need was in respect of mortgages and the protection of the defaulting mortgagor. It was finally met in 1837 when a Court of Chancery was established with the Governor as Chancellor but with provision for a judge to exercise his powers with the title of Vice-Chancellor. The same Court of Appeal as was prescribed for the Court of King's Bench was to do service in equity appeals.

A reorganisation of the judicial system of Upper Canada took place in 1849 when a Court of Common Pleas was established as a court of civil and criminal jurisdiction co-ordinate with the then Queen's Bench. In addition, a Court of Error and Appeal was created to be manned by the judges of the Courts of Queen's Bench, Chancery and Common Pleas.[32]

Apart from changes in the composition of the courts, the system as it stood after 1849 continued until the Judicature Act 1881. Earlier suggestions to give equitable jurisdiction to the common law courts, as had been done in Nova Scotia, had been rejected, but even after the Judicature Act, with its provision for concurrent application of law and equity with the latter to prevail in case of variance between them, the separate divisions of Queen's Bench, Chancery and Common Pleas were retained as constituents of the High Court of Justice and with their work to be assigned according to Rules of Court. A completely separate Court of Appeal under that name was

[31] Falconbridge, "Law and Equity in Upper Canada" (1914) 34 C.L.T. 1130.

[32] 1849 (Can.), c. 63.

established. A fourth division, Exchequer, was added to the High Court of Justice in 1903. The division system has now disappeared and Ontario's superior court system consists of an undifferentiated High Court of Justice and a Court of Appeal.[33] That of the other common law Provinces is, with a few minor exceptions, the same.[34]

The concentration of this narrative upon the development of the superior courts has been at the expense of attention to the system of county and district courts which exist in the common law Provinces, and of attention to various kinds of provincially appointed judicial officers, such as justice of the peace, magistrates and provincial judges. By constitutional prescription in 1867 the judges of the superior courts of the Provinces and of the county and district courts thereof are appointed and paid by the national government. This is, of course, also true of the judges of the Supreme Court of Canada which was established in 1875, and now exercises ultimate civil and criminal appellate jurisdiction. The constitution does not preclude provincial appointment of inferior judicial officers to administer provincial legislation respecting matters not constitutionally within the jurisdiction of the superior, county and district courts; and, indeed, these provincially appointed officers may also be invested by the

[33] This has been the case since 1931; see now the Judicature Act, R.S.O. 1960, c. 197, s. 3.

[34] I have already referred to the separate Chancery Court in Prince Edward Island. In New Brunswick, there was a separate Chancery Division of the Supreme Court (as well as a Queen's Bench Division and an Appeal Division) until 1966, when the Chancery Division was absorbed by the Queen's Bench Division: see 1966 (N.B.), c. 70. In Prince Edward Island and in Newfoundland the superior court judges sit *en banc* as had been the case in Nova Scotia until 1966 when an Act of 1962, c. 18, was proclaimed and under which the Supreme Court was to consist of an Appeal Division and a Trial Division.

Parliament of Canada with administration of federal legislation. The prime example is the central role played by provincial magistrates and judges in the administration of the Criminal Code.

The Legal Profession

Although the legal profession is self-governing in Canada, it is so in a sense quite different from the self-government of the Inns of Court in England. Statutes incorporating Law Societies exist in the various Provinces, and they delineate the governing organs of the profession, and the powers, especially in relation to discipline, that may be exercised over members. In some of the Provinces, the head of the Law Society is the Treasurer, and in most the governing council are the Benchers, terms that do have an Inns of Court flavour.[35] Not only do the Law Societies control admission to practice,[36] but they are empowered

[35] Treasurer is the term used in Ontario, British Columbia and Newfoundland; the other common law Provinces use the term President; in Quebec, the head of the Bar of the Province of Quebec is the Batonnier. In New Brunswick and in Nova Scotia, the profession is organised in a Barristers' Society; it is the Law Society in the other common law Provinces; in Quebec the Order of Advocates is the professional body incorporated as the Bar of the Province of Quebec.

[36] I have not dealt with the history of the admission of women to the practice of law; they were admitted in most of Canada before they were acceptable in England, but not without a struggle in some Provinces: see *Re Mabel French* (1905) 37 N.B.R. 359; the decision was overruled by a retrospective statute 1906 (N.B.), c. 5. Clara Brett Martin, the first woman to be admitted to the Bar in Canada if not in the British Empire at the time, was enrolled as a student at law by the Law Society of Upper Canada in 1893 after having been previously refused and after legislation was passed to assist in the matter; she was admitted to practice in 1897. *Bibb* v. *The Law Society* [1914] 1 Ch. 286 states the common law position similar to the *French* case, *supra.* The disqualification has now disappeared in Canada.

to regulate and even administer legal education. Happily, this last-mentioned authority is now prudently and circumspectly asserted in collaboration with and recognition of university law schools which exist in all the Provinces save Prince Edward Island and Newfoundland.

There are other Inns of Court influences which remain. It cannot be said in Canada, as is the case in England, that call to the Bar is not, strictly speaking, a call to the Bar of the court but a call to the Bar of the provincial integrated " Inn "; nonetheless the right of audience in the courts depends on the Law Society's certification. Similarly, such certification qualifies solicitors, even though they may also be obliged to be formally enrolled by the courts.

Again, judges are in a number of Provinces declared to be visitors of their Law Societies, but this is without the substance reflected in the recent Gray's Inn proceeding reported in *Re S.*[37] The dignity is statutory in Canada, and only in Newfoundland is any express authority conferred upon the visitors, that of giving required approval to rules of the Law Society with respect to the qualification of solicitors.[38] Elsewhere, either nothing is said about the powers of the visitors or there is an express withdrawal, in favour of the Benchers, of any powers that the visitors might have, in their character as such, in matters of discipline.[39] Their powers of review in other matters that

37 See Law Society Act 1956 (Man.), c. 39, s. 32; Law Society Act, R.S.Nfld. 1952, c. 115, s. 4; Law Society Act, R.S.O. 1960, c. 207, s. 3; Legal Profession Act, R.S.S. 1965, c. 301, s. 7; *Re S.* is reported in [1969] 1 All E.R. 949.

38 Law Society Act, R.S.Nfld. 1952, c. 115, ss. 35 and 58.

39 Law Society Act, R.S.O. 1960, c. 207, s. 49; Legal Profession Act, R.S.S. 1965, c. 301, s. 66. It would appear that the vesting of disciplinary power in the Benchers with a right of appeal to the court,

are the concern of the Law Societies are doubtful, but there is one precedent from Manitoba which concerns a resigned judge who cited the Law Society to appear before the judges as visitors and succeeded, in a majority decision, in vindicating his right, under the existing legislation, to be called to the Bar without any fee.[40]

Public and collective accountability of the profession has been reflected in the past decade in provision by a growing number of Law Societies of a contributory compensation fund out of which, on a purely discretionary basis however, individual clients who have been wronged by their solicitors through misappropriation or conversion of property may obtain some reimbursement on application to the particular Law Society.[41] Again, Law Societies have also been charged with the formulation and administration of legal aid programmes and, as in Ontario, have been entrusted with the spending of public money voted for that purpose.[42]

The nomenclature for the branches of the legal profession in the common law Provinces is the English one, but the organisation of the profession for practice has been and remains different. The terms barrister, attorney, solicitor and proctor had institutional meaning until, following the example of legislation in the United Kingdom, they were reduced to the two of barrister and solicitor, save that in Prince Edward Island, which still has a Court of Chancery, the formal difference between attorney and solicitor is still

which is common, is incompatible with any surviving jurisdiction in the visitors.

[40] See *Re the Hon. James A. Miller* (1886) 3 Man.R. 367; Marsh, "Visitors and their Jurisdiction" (1895) 15 C.L.T. 173.

[41] This is the case in Alberta, British Columbia, Nova Scotia, Ontario and Saskatchewan.

[42] Legal Aid Act 1966 (Ont.), c. 80.

recognised. The uniting of the functions of barrister and solicitor in the same persons had its impact upon legal education in Canada which, in any event, had taken a turn by the end of the first quarter of the 20th century towards the American scheme of professional education and training in university law schools.

In Quebec, the separate branches of advocate and notary have some but no exact similarity to barrister and solicitor. There is a small overlap of function, but a person cannot be advocate and notary at the same time. This is as far as any comparison with the United Kingdom can be carried. The advocate is entitled to designate himself barrister and solicitor; and, indeed, he now combines in himself functions of the offices of barrister, attorney, solicitor and proctor, as they were known in the 19th century.[43] The notary, fully a member of the legal profession by training and by assigned powers, was the only legal practitioner in the earliest days of New France which, by deliberate policy, had no advocates. It was after the British presence that legal work was divided between advocates and notaries, with the latter being assigned exclusive authority, as their main function, to give authentic character to deeds and certified copies, which are judicially recognised as acts of public officers.[44]

Notwithstanding the fusion of the two branches of the profession from the very beginning of the administration of justice in what is now common law Canada (and in part in Quebec), practices dependent on the English separation were nonetheless recognised. Thus, until legislation and

[43] The Bar Act 1966–67 (Que.), c. 77.

[44] See Common, "The Role of the Notary in the Province of Quebec" (1958) 36 Can. Bar Rev. 333; Rowat, "The Notarial Profession in the Province of Quebec" (1924) 2 Can. Bar Rev. 391, 460.

authorised prescription of tariffs of fees led to a change, the common law rule prevailed in the common law Provinces that fees for counsel work were not recoverable by action. True, dicta in the case law leaned to a rejection of the English rule as inapplicable to the Canadian situation, but effective rejection had to await a legislative basis. The civil law of Quebec was different; under it, a member of the Bar could sue for his professional fees for barrister's work; and even on a *quantum meruit* assessment if no fixed contractual arrangement had been made.[45]

Does the lawyer in Canada, whose fees as counsel are subject to taxation and who can now recover them in legal proceedings, enjoy the *Rondel* v. *Worsley* immunity of an English barrister? [46] There is no doubt that negligence in the performance of solicitor's work will attract liability, and in some Provinces the contracting out of liability for negligence is expressly forbidden to a solicitor.[47] Can or should a distinction be drawn in the case of a solicitor, who also acts as counsel in the case, between his liability in the one character and his immunity in the other? And what of the position of counsel who is instructed by a solicitor?

What case law there is in the common law Provinces—and it is scanty—indicates that where a lawyer acts both as solicitor and counsel his negligence in the latter character

45 *The Queen* v. *Doutre* (1882) 6 S.C.R. 342, affirmed (1884) 9 App.Cas. 745.

46 [1969] 1 A.C. 191. See the discussion by Roxburgh in (1968) 84 L.Q.R. 178, 513.

47 For example, The Legal Professions Act, R.S.B.C. 1960, c. 214, s. 108 (3); Solicitors Act, R.S.O. 1960, c. 378, s. 53; Alberta Rules of Court, r. 620 (1).

will be as actionable as his negligence as solicitor.[48] Difficult though it may be to raise errors of judgment into negligence, it is still more difficult to separate what a person knows or does or ought reasonably to know or do as a solicitor from what he knows or does or ought reasonably to know or do as counsel, where he fills both roles.

Nor do I think that any rule of immunity is justified where a person acts as counsel only, whether in a particular case or as a matter of general practice. The rules of conduct that in England govern the relations between barristers and solicitors have no meaning in Canada. Lawyers here are generally both barristers and solicitors, and certainly belong to the same Law Society. It was possible in Ontario until 1964 to be admitted as a solicitor without being called to the Bar; since that date the rules of the Law Society of Upper Canada provide for admission in both capacities or not at all. In sum, *Rondel* v. *Worsley* is based on considerations which have no Canadian relevance.

Legislation in the Canadian Provinces now permits fee arrangements between members of the legal profession and their clients which would be champertous under the English common law. It is not only that lawyers may bargain for remuneration upon another or higher scale than that allowed by tariffs of fees; that they may be employed on a yearly salary basis; that they may contract to be paid on a commission or percentage basis for non-contentious business and for conveyancing, subject to taxing officer appraisal [49];

[48] See *Leslie* v. *Ball* (1863) 22 U.C.Q.B. 512; *cf. Wade* v. *Ball* (1870) 20 U.C.C.P. 302; and see Catzman, Note (1968) 46 Can. Bar Rev. 505, taking a view different from that of the text.

[49] For some background, see *Re Solicitor* (1912) 3 O.W.N. 1274; *Faulkner* v. *Grand Junction Ry.* (1883) 4 O.R. 350.

but in some Provinces, contingent fee arrangements for a share in the fruits of litigation are permitted on observance of prescribed conditions. Manitoba has had legislation to this effect since 1890.[50] Legislation enacted in 1967 and supplemented by Rules of Court provides for such fees in Alberta.[51] A by-law of the Bar of Quebec adopted in 1967 places a limit of 30 per cent. upon contingent fee arrangements.[52] In Saskatchewan, contingent fee arrangements may be made in respect of damage claims to a limit of 15 per cent. on settlement before trial and 20 per cent. if the action proceeds to trial.[53] The incompatibility of this provision in the Law Society's Tariff of Costs with a canon of legal ethics forbidding the acquisition of any interest in the subject-matter of litigation by purchase or otherwise, except as by law expressly sanctioned, was overcome by a Bencher's ruling in 1968 that the canon was to be interpreted as subject to the tariff provision. In British Columbia, there has been cautious recognition of the contingent fee in contentious matters if related to the measure of an earned fee and if not a blatant division of the spoils.[54] Judicial approbation was given in New Brunswick in 1962 to a contingent fee of this character.[55] Apart from special requirements for the enforceability of such fees, as for

[50] See on this point *Thomson* v. *Wishart* (1910) 19 Man.R. 340; and see 1890 (Man.), c. 2, s. 37.

[51] Judicature Act, R.S.A. 1955, c. 164, s. 38a, enacted by 1967, c. 42; rr. 615, 616 and 618 of the Rules of the Court, effective January 1, 1969.

[52] By-law 1, s. 87, of the By-laws of the Bar of Quebec, adopted October 20, 1967.

[53] Law Society's Extra-Judicial Tariff of Costs, Item II.

[54] *Cf. Monteith* v. *Calladine* (1964) 49 W.W.R. 641.

[55] *Hogan* v. *Hello et al.* (1962), a judgment of Michaud C.J.Q.B. of March 14, 1962, unreported.

example in Manitoba and Alberta, there is the general overriding power of the taxing officer to which contingent fees of all kinds are subject.

Perhaps another incongruity, and one which has survived in shabby imitation of its English exemplar, is appointments of counsel learned in the law. Save for some effort at control of numbers in British Columbia and in Prince Edward Island,[56] present Canadian practice in conferring the distinction of Queen's Counsel exhibits adoption of the form of the English tradition while shedding its substance. This was not originally the case, at least in Upper Canada. Apart from an abortive attempt in 1815 at an appointment as King's Counsel of a 23-year-old man, then only a few months at the Bar,[57] only three such appointments (all in 1838) were made in the nearly 50-year period that Upper Canada was a separate colony. Thereafter, the appointments became more frequent (they had been more numerous in Lower Canada), and the legal periodicals of the latter half of the 19th century began to carry the criticisms which are still heard about the indiscriminate and politically motivated nature of the appointments.

When fifty-eight Q.C.s were gazetted in Ontario in 1899, a journal comment was that "the list should have been much larger or else much smaller."[58] J. S. Ewart, a distinguished Canadian lawyer who practised in Manitoba in the late 19th century and whose law texts enjoyed an

[56] Queen's Counsel Act, R.S.B.C. 1960, c. 326, am. 1964, c. 49; The Legal Profession Act, R.S.P.E.I. 1951, c. 84, s. 23. In the other Provinces, there is, in general, a requirement of a specified minimum length of time at the Bar.

[57] Riddell, "The First and Futile Attempt to Create a King's Counsel in Upper Canada" (1920) 40 C.L.T. 92.

[58] (1899) 19 C.L.T. 257.

international reputation, remarked in 1884 that " the practice of singling out, from time to time, certain barristers for invidious distinction should have been abolished together with patents of monopoly—that is centuries ago." [59] The " invidious distinction " was not, of course, confined to lawyers who specialised in counsel work; solicitors and salaried lawyers employed by business corporations were also anointed. Thus 188 Ontario lawyers were appointed King's Counsel in 1908, and this list resulted in a total of 354 since 1900. " ' Silk ' has ceased to be an honour," said a critical editorial.[60] There is nothing new to report on this question in the more than sixty years that have since elapsed. Happily, there is no Gresham's law to contend with; the bad appointments do not drive out the good ones. I may add that there has been no emulation in Canada of the English practice that a junior must accompany a Queen's Counsel leader. In the early days, the scarcity of resources, if nothing else, would not permit it. When Queen's Counsel do appear with a junior, it is a matter of convenience or expediency but not of recognised obligation.

In all the Provinces, the Queen's Counsel exchanges his stuff gown for a silk one and in most of them he is called to plead within the Bar, that is inside a railing (which brings him closer to the Bench) rather than outside it. This piling of empty form upon empty form has been discarded in British Columbia and in Saskatchewan; there is no Bar, and all counsel, whether formally designated as learned or not, plead from the same vantage point before the court.

Queen's Counsel appointments became an issue of

59 (1884) 1 Man.L.J. 177. Ewart had just been created a Q.C.
60 (1908) 44 C.L.J. 49.

federal-provincial contention in the last quarter of the 19th century, becoming enmeshed in a consideration of Crown prerogative and the survival in a federal state of the notion of the indivisibility of the Crown. The matter reached the Privy Council in an Ontario appeal in 1897, and that body sustained the ruling of the court below that the Ontario legislature could competently vest in the provincial Lieutenant-Governor power to designate members of the Ontario Bar as Queen's Counsel; and moreover that it could authorise him to issue patents of precedence of members of the Bar.[61] The position in Canada now is that appointments as Queen's Counsel, an office whose duties (said the Privy Council) "are almost as insubstantial as its emoluments," are competent to federal authorities in relation to practice in federal courts as they are to provincial authorities in relation to practice in provincial courts. Federal appointments of counsel learned in the law have been infrequent when compared to the torrent in the Provinces. Key civil servants employed in a legal capacity have generally been accorded the honour, and, occasionally, a law-trained Minister.

Unlike the situation in the United States, there is no separate federal Bar; Canada has not chosen to establish admission requirements or to formalise rights of audience before federal courts but has simply provided by statute that persons qualified to practise in any Province may appear as of right in any federal court.[62]

Formal court dress in Canada as in the United Kingdom includes gown, wing collar and bands. The black gown is

[61] *Att.-Gen. Can.* v. *Att.-Gen. Ont.* [1898] A.C. 247.

[62] Supreme Court Act, R.S.C. 1952, c. 259, ss. 22–24; Exchequer Court Act, R.S.C. 1952, c. 98, ss. 14–16.

generally worn by judges, as by counsel (a silk gown with squared off back, if a Queen's Counsel); but in a few superior courts, for example, in the Supreme Court of Canada and in the High Court of Justice of Ontario, the judges also have more resplendent robes. The judges of the Supreme Court of Canada wear their red robes on ceremonial occasions, at the opening of session and on the hearing of appeals in capital cases. The Ontario trial judges wear their gowns on ceremonial occasions and at trials.

Wigs were apparently worn by judges and barristers in Nova Scotia into the 19th century and the judges there wore them into the second quarter but not the barristers. The certain record of their use in Canadian courts is in those of British Columbia where the practice was brought to an end by legislation in 1905. That legislation converted a permissive provision in 1904 into an express prohibition against the wearing of wigs.[63] A chronicler of the period remarked of the British Columbia penchant for wigs that "the $50 required to buy a wig could secure a dozen useful textbooks, and the brain would be cooler."[64] It is reported that an Irish barrister in the middle of the 19th century brought a wig from Dublin and wore it in Toronto but "he was subjected to many practical jokes in one of which the wig disappeared forever."[65]

Another tradition that was not originally adopted in Canada was the English form of address and entitlement of the superior court judges. They were "Your Honour"

63 Supreme Court Act 1903–1904 (B.C.), c. 15, s. 112, as amended by 1905 (B.C.), c. 16, s. 2.

64 Hamilton, *Osgoode Hall Reminiscences of the Bench and Bar* (1904) at pp. 119–120.

65 *Ibid.* at p. 121.

and " His Honour " in Upper Canada until the second quarter of the 19th century.[66] This mode of address survived in New Brunswick into the 20th century notwithstanding a formal resolution of the Barristers' Society of that Province in the last quarter of the 19th to have the judges of its superior courts addressed as " My Lord," as was by then the custom in Ontario and elsewhere in Canada.[67] So far as I have been able to determine, the present-day salutation of " Your Lordship " has no formal basis; it rests on exaggerated courtesy, and perhaps on an assumed enhancement of prestige to mark the superior courts off from the inferior county and district courts whose presiding officers are " Their Honours." I cannot forbear to note that a judge of the High Court of Australia is " His Honour " despite the fact that he may be knighted. A judge of the Supreme Court of the United States is also " His Honour " without the redeeming possibility of a title. It may strike others, as it strikes me, to be pretentious for Canadian society, which rejects titles of honour in the formal gift of the British monarch, that any class of judges should be addressed as " My Lord."

I do not think that it is an offsetting consideration that in Quebec and in Ontario presiding officers of summary courts, who would be called magistrates in the English system, are now designated provincial judges. His Worship has become His Honour; and, clearly, one of the purposes

[66] Riddell, *Upper Canada Sketches* (1922), p. 24; there are other similar references in Riddell's writings: see *The Courts of Upper Canada* (1926) at p. 159.

[67] Lawrence, *The Judges of New Brunswick and Their Times* (1907) at p. 524. Hamilton, *Osgoode Hall Reminiscences of the Bench and Bar* (1904) at p. 122 states that this form of address did not come into use in Quebec until 1901.

of the change was to enhance the prestige of and attraction of appointment to a Bench which has the widest contact with the public.

The judges of the superior courts in Canada do have one formal titular distinction. Approval was given by His Majesty King George V on May 21, 1913, for the use and recognition of the title " Honourable " in the case of judges of the Supreme Court of Canada, of the Exchequer Court of Canada, and of the superior courts of the Provinces, during their tenure of office.[68] Upon retirement, permission may be given (and it invariably is) for continued recognition of that designation.

The received oral tradition in the presentation of argument has remained strong in Canada. Written briefs at the appellate level are intended simply to indicate the direction of the oral advocacy. There are no formal limitations of time but only the informal yardstick of judicial patience. There has been no discernible disposition, even in the more heavily burdened appellate courts, such as the Supreme Court of Canada and the Court of Appeal of Ontario, to lean to the American example of written argument and strict time limits on oral presentation.

Law clerks have recently been provided for each of the judges of Canada's final court, and similar assistance on a less generous scale has been given in Ontario for almost a decade. Alleviation of the pressure from the increasing volume of appellate work has been managed by having the courts sit in panels; for example, three-judge courts in

[68] The title " Honourable " was in use for superior court judges before this approval, but I have been unable to discover any earlier formal basis for it. The 1913 provision is in the Statutes of Canada for 1914, 4–5 Geo. 5, p. XV.

Ontario which has a total complement of ten Justices of Appeal, and five- or seven-judge courts at the Supreme Court of Canada level. Although two or even three courts can sit concurrently in Ontario (and two is usually the case), this is not possible with the nine-judge complement of the Supreme Court of Canada when five is a quorum. In any event, there is a dilution of judgment involved in a five-judge panel with a shifting composition (which is the usual situation), or even in a seven-judge panel of the Supreme Court of Canada, and this is undesirable in a final court. It would be the preferable course, if the work load for a full court or a seven-judge court should otherwise be unmanageable, to confine access as of right to constitutional matters and other public law issues, subject to the court's own wishes on the hearing of appeals in other cases.

2

ENGLISH LAW IN CANADIAN COURTS: THE JUDICIAL OFFICE IN CANADA

THE courts in Britain's Canadian colonies began their work in the 18th century not only with a received or imposed body of substantive law and procedure, albeit with some adaptation to local conditions, but also, and understandably, with either an imported or an untrained judiciary.[1] The first Chief Justice of Nova Scotia, Jonathan Belcher, appointed in 1754 and again in 1761 (there was then no applicable "demise of the Crown" legislation), on both occasions during pleasure, was a son of the Governor of Massachusetts, Harvard-educated and a member of the Middle Temple. He, as his counterparts later in the other colonies, was a member of the Governor's Council. Act of Settlement tenure did not govern the appointment of colonial judges; and the issues of their security of tenure and of their dissociation from the executive and legislative branches of government remained to be worked out in the 19th century.

The American colonies contributed significantly to the Canadian judiciary after the revolution. George Duncan Ludlow, the first Chief Justice of New Brunswick, appointed in 1784, had been a New York judge; Peter Livius, the

1 I have drawn on various sources for what follows in this section, including Townshend, "Historical Account of the Courts of Judicature in Nova Scotia" (1899) 19 C.L.T. 87, 142; Lawrence, *The Judges of New Brunswick and Their Times* (1907); Riddell, *The Courts of Upper Canada* (1926); Buchanan, *The Bench and Bar of Lower Canada* (1925).

third Chief Justice of Quebec had been a judge in New Hampshire; and his successor as Chief Justice of Quebec, William Smith, had been Solicitor-General of New York and in 1780 held the formal but empty title of Chief Justice of New York. The early history of the judiciary in the maritime Provinces and in Quebec shows the large extent to which its members came from loyalist families that had made their way to England and thence to British North America or had gone directly to those colonies.

In Quebec, the first two Chief Justices of the Court of King's Bench under Governor Murray's Ordinance were William Gregory and William Hey, both English barristers. By contrast, the first judges of the Courts of Common Pleas had no legal qualifications; for example, Adam Mabane, a celebrated name by reason of long executive and judicial service, was an army surgeon; Francis Mounier and Thomas Dunn were merchants; and John Fraser and Jean Claude Panet were soldiers. Lawyers were later introduced as judges in this court, and one of the ablest was William Dummer Powell, Boston-born and English-trained, a member of the Middle Temple, who capped his career by becoming Chief Justice of Upper Canada in 1816. He was appointed in 1789 as a judge of the Court of Common Pleas in one of the new districts of Quebec and in 1794 became the first puisne judge of the new Court of King's Bench of Upper Canada.

In the meantime he continued to sit in the Court of Common Pleas—the only one of the four judges in the respective court districts who was a lawyer—until its abolition. William Osgoode, a member of Lincoln's Inn, had received a royal appointment in late 1791 as Chief Justice of Upper Canada; and, as is well known, his name was given to the seat of the superior courts of the Province in Toronto although his judicial service was comparatively short. He made his contribution as a member of the Executive Council and as draftsman of important statutes; for example, the Act introducing English law in 1792, and the Judicature Act of 1794 which launched Upper Canada's judicial system. He himself did not, however, sit in the Court of King's Bench created by the latter Act. By the time of its enactment he had obtained an appointment as Chief Justice of Lower Canada, then a better paid and more highly regarded judicial office. His two immediate successors as Chief Justice of Upper Canada, Elmsley and Allcock, both from England and members respectively of the Middle Temple and Lincoln's Inn, followed him in turn as successive Chief Justices of Lower Canada.

Indeed, judicial musical chairs were played in the various Canadian colonies in the late 18th and early 19th centuries. Two of the Chief Justices of Prince Edward Island, Cochrane and Thorpe, came to Upper Canada as puisne judges of the Court of King's Bench. Thomas Tremlett, without legal training, became Chief Justice of Newfoundland and later Chief Justice of Prince Edward Island. John Duport, the first Chief Justice of Prince Edward Island in 1770, had been a Nova Scotia judge. Edward James Jarvis, whose appointment as a judge in New Brunswick, where he was a member of the Bar, was not confirmed, obtained a judicial appointment in Malta and in 1827 became Chief Justice of Prince Edward Island. James Monk, first Chief Justice of the Montreal District in 1794, came from Nova Scotia where he had been Solicitor-General, and he was for a considerable time Attorney-General of Quebec and then of Lower Canada. William

Campbell, although born in Scotland, studied law in Nova Scotia, and became a puisne judge in Upper Canada in 1811 (and Chief Justice in 1825) after having been Attorney-General of Cape Breton, which was then a separate colony and did not become re-annexed to Nova Scotia until 1820. Robert S. Jameson, who became the first Vice-Chancellor of the Court of Chancery established in Upper Canada in 1837, had been a Judge in the island of Dominica in the West Indies and later was appointed Attorney-General of Upper Canada, the last of such appointments by the British Government. John Hamilton Gray, educated in Nova Scotia, and at one time Attorney-General of New Brunswick and Speaker of its Legislative Assembly, sat in the first Canadian Parliament after Confederation, and in 1872 was appointed to the Supreme Court of British Columbia when that Province was already part of Canada.

Under applicable provisions of the British North America Act, federally appointed judges of the courts of the Provinces were to be selected from the Bars of the respective Provinces and Gray's appointment was quite unusual although he was called to the provincial Bar before taking his seat on the Bench. If not offensive to the letter of the Constitution, it was to the spirit and to the legal profession of British Columbia. Gray's appointment was not, however, a lonely precedent. In 1883, Thomas Wardlaw Taylor, then Master in Chancery in Ontario, was appointed a puisne judge in Manitoba and in 1887 became Chief Justice of the Province.

Independence of The Judiciary

Appointments of the judges of the courts in the Canadian colonies as well as the establishment of courts were originally in the hands of the British authorities as matters of the royal prerogative.[2] Delegation of this authority to local Governors was effected by order-in-council or by proclamation or even through their commissions and instructions, but this did not mean relinquishment of ultimate control. General policy was laid down for all colonial governors from 1754 on that judicial appointments to colonial courts were to be at pleasure only. The Quebec Act 1774 preserved the royal prerogative of appointment which survived as well the establishment of representative legislative assemblies and the conferring of power upon the local legislature to create courts. It even had local statutory recognition, as witness a measure of the Nova Scotia legislature in 1848 under which judicial appointments (although during good behaviour) by the Governor became and remained effective unless the royal pleasure was otherwise, or was expressed in a superseding appointment.[3] With the coming of responsible government, the power to appoint judges passed to the local Ministry upon whose advice the Governor was obliged to act; and thereafter as one chronicler put it, the appointment of a judge by the influence of Downing Street was rendered virtually impossible.[4]

The concern to make judicial appointments a matter of local responsibility was matched by a concern to give the judges security of tenure and to remove them from partisan political involvement that was a risk of membership in

2 For a full account of the developments to judicial independence, see Lederman, " Independence of the Judiciary " (1956) 34 Can. Bar Rev. 769, 1139.

3 1848 (N.S.), c. 21, s. 5.

4 Lawrence, *op. cit.*, note 1 at p. 370.

executive and legislative bodies. A statute of Upper Canada in 1834 prescribed tenure during good behaviour for its superior court judges, and the principle was extended to the Queen's Bench judges in Lower Canada by an 1843 statute of the then united Province of Canada. Other superior court judges were embraced in legislation in 1849 applicable in both Canadas.[5] Similar legislation was enacted in Nova Scotia in 1848.[6]

With Confederation in 1867, and the appointing power respecting judges of the superior, county and district courts of the Provinces vested by the Constitution in the federal government, tenure during good behaviour was constitutionally guaranteed but only to the superior court judges. A constitutional amendment in 1960 translated the theoretical lifetime appointment into compulsory retirement at the age of 75.[7] The judges of the county and district courts of the Provinces, and as well the judges of the Supreme Court of Canada (whose establishment was merely authorised by the Constitution and not declared thereby) enjoy the same guarantee of tenure under the same limitation of age through federal statute.[8]

Even before security of tenure was formally established for the King's Bench judges of Upper Canada, pressures to dissociate them from the Executive and Legislative Councils—part of the drive for responsible government—bore fruit. Lower Canada acted early in this matter by providing in 1811 that King's Bench judges were ineligible

[5] 1834 (U.C.), c. 2; 1843 (Can.), c. 15; 1849 (Can.), cc. 37, 38, 63.
[6] 1848 (N.S.), c. 21, ss. 2 and 3.
[7] 1960 (U.K.), c. 2, replacing s. 99 of the British North America Act and effective March 1, 1961.
[8] The Judges Act, R.S.C. 1952, c. 159, s. 26 (1); the Supreme Court Act, R.S.C. 1952, c. 259, s. 9 (2).

to be members of the Legislative Assembly.[9] In 1831 the Chief Justice of Upper Canada ceased to sit on the Executive Council and retired from the Legislative Council in 1838. Some analogy, which could only have been faint, was thought to exist to the position of the Lord Chancellor in the United Kingdom, as a member and presiding officer in the Upper House, and thus to support in principle membership of the Chief Justice in colonial Upper Houses. However, the analogy proved unconvincing. For a few years after 1838, first a puisne judge and then the Vice-Chancellor of the Court of Chancery became members and speakers of the Legislative Council of Upper Canada, but the whole matter of judges in the Province of Canada sitting in any legislative bodies was laid to rest by disqualifying legislation in 1857.[10]

It may be noted that the common law principle, and the theory underlying it, that precluded membership of English common law judges in the House of Commons was not applicable to the colonies; and some colonial judges did, while in judicial office, become elected members of the Legislative Assembly.[11] The comprehensive settlement of the matter in the Province of Canada came before the similar disqualifying legislation in the United Kingdom in 1873 which was necessary to cover the Chancery judges who, unless they were peers, were not caught by the common law principle. Other colonies in British North America likewise closed the door earlier to judges' membership in legislative bodies. Nova Scotia acted in 1848, as did Prince

[9] 1811 (L.C.), c. 4.

[10] 1857 (Can.), c. 22.

[11] See Riddell, "Judges in the Parliament of Upper Canada" (1919) 3 Minn.L.Rev. 163, 244. The common law principle referred to in the text is discussed by Lederman, *op. cit.*, note 2.

Edward Island; and New Brunswick, Newfoundland, British Columbia (on the eve of its union with Canada) followed suit. Manitoba legislated to the same effect, as did Alberta and Saskatchewan after they became separate Provinces.[12]

The statutory preclusion of membership in legislative bodies also meant, in accordance with principles of responsible government, that judges would not be members of a Ministry. Indeed, the present statutory prohibitions in federal and provincial legislation are reinforced by the Judges Act, under which federally appointed judges are commanded, subject to stated exceptions, to devote themselves entirely to their judicial duties.[13] Similar provincial legislation exists with respect to provincially appointed judges.[14]

JURY TRIAL IN CANADA

The original veneration of trial by jury, especially in civil cases, in the courts of the Canadian colonies is illustrated by the terms of the second statute enacted by the new legislature of Upper Canada in 1792. Reciting that " trial by jury has long been established and approved in our Mother Country and is one of the chief benefits to be attained by a free constitution," it went on to prescribe that all issues of fact in any action " shall be tried and determined by the unanimous verdict of twelve jurors . . . summoned and taken conformably to the law and custom of England."

[12] See 1848 (N.S.), c. 21, s. 2; 1848 (P.E.I.), c. 29, s. 6; R.S.N.B. 1877, c. 4, s. 27; R.S.Nfld. 1872, c. 6; the Constitution Act 1871 (B.C.), No. 147, s. 8; 1875 (Man.), c. 2; Legislative Assembly Act 1909 (Alta.), c. 2, s. 9; Legislative Assembly Act 1906 (Sask.), c. 2, s. 12.

[13] R.S.C. 1952, c. 159, ss. 37–39.

[14] See, for example, Provincial Courts Act 1968 (Ont.), c. 103, s. 12.

The small debt courts aside, this remained the rule until changes in the English procedure, beginning with the Common Law Procedure Act of 1854 (which first gave the power, in limited circumstances, to try common law cases without a jury) made their influence felt in Canada. Ontario made a more severe inroad in 1868 on the civil jury than had the United Kingdom to that date by providing that all civil actions should be tried by a judge alone unless a jury notice was served by either party; and even where this was done, the parties at the trial could agree to go on without a jury; but the right was reserved to the trial judge to direct a jury trial. Ontario in 1873 anticipated to a degree United Kingdom legislation ten years later by preserving jury trial (subject to waiver by the parties) in a specified number of tort actions including defamation, false imprisonment and malicious prosecution. Later developments in the United Kingdom, culminating in section 6 of the Administration of Justice (Miscellaneous Provisions) Act 1933, overtook the Ontario law and that in the other Provinces.[15]

The developments in the Canadian Provinces proceeded on several fronts. The requirement of unanimity, which still obtains in Canada in criminal prosecutions tried with a jury, was abated. The number " twelve " lost its magic. In most Provinces, discretion was vested in the court or a judge to order trial without a jury notwithstanding the service of a jury notice; indeed, with some exceptions, the prevailing rule became no jury unless one was demanded. Correlatively, power was left in some Provinces to the trial judge to direct a jury trial notwithstanding that a jury was

[15] See, generally, Devlin, *Trial by Jury* (3rd impression, 1966), p. 129 *et seq.*

not originally sought.[16] Finally, with a few exceptions, the Provinces have made women eligible for jury service.[17]

Historically, jury trial was introduced into Quebec with the establishment, by Governor Murray's Ordinance, of the Court of King's Bench, with civil and criminal jurisdiction exercisable "agreeable to the laws of England." In the inferior Court of Common Pleas, also created at that time, jury trial could be had on the demand of either party. The civil jury disappeared with the Quebec Act 1774 by which the French civil law was restored, but it was re-introduced for commercial contract cases and for damage claims for personal wrongs by an Ordinance of 1785. The substance of this Ordinance in respect of jury trial continued in force in the Province of Quebec under its Code of Civil Procedure, which also comprehended the extension of jury trial in 1829 to claims of damage to movable property. Moreover, until 1965 it remained the law, as first ordained in 1785, that the jury should consist of twelve persons of whom nine could bring in a verdict.

The new Quebec Code of Civil Procedure, promulgated in 1965, reduced the number on the jury from twelve to six, of whom four may bring in a verdict. Jury trial may be

16 The various provincial enactments in this matter are as follows: Jury Act, R.S.A. 1955, c. 165, ss. 28 (am. 1966, c. 45, s. 7) and 32; Jury Act, R.S.B.C. 1960, c. 202, ss. 47 and 49; Jury Act, R.S.M. 1954, c. 130, s. 67; Queen's Bench Act, R.S.M. 1954, c. 52, s. 65; Jury Act, R.S.N.B. 1952, c. 121, am. 1954, c. 50, ss. 24 and 30; Judicature Act, R.S.Nfld. 1952, c. 114, ss. 39 and 87; Juries Act 1967 (N.S.), c. 156, s. 54; Judicature Act 1950 (N.S.), s. 42; Jurors Act, R.S.O. 1960, c. 199, s. 71; Judicature Act, R.S.O. 1960, c. 197, s. 55 *et seq.*; Jury Act, R.S.P.E.I. 1951, c. 81, ss. 19 and 35; Judicature Act, R.S.P.E.I. 1951, c. 79, s. 32; Jury Act, R.S.Q. 1964, c. 26, s. 58; Quebec Code of Civil Procedure, art. 430 *et seq.*; Jury Act, R.S.S. 1965, c. 79, s. 17; Queen's Bench Act, R.S.S. 1965, c. 73, ss. 68 and 69.

17 Quebec and Newfoundland are the exceptions.

sought (subject to the court's power to refuse it) if the amount claimed exceeds $5,000 (the amount was formerly $1,000) and is for damages in a personal injury or fatal accidents action, or for damage to corporeal property resulting from an offence or quasi-offence (to use the words of Article 332). As before, an all-French or all-English jury is the rule, depending on the one or the other being the language of the parties. The mixed jury, composed of half English-speaking and half French-speaking persons, which was provided for in legislation of 1852, has also survived; and now, as then, may be had when sought by either party to the action if one speaks French and the other English. A corporation when a party is now also allowed to ask for a mixed jury.

The size of the civil jury in the common law Provinces does not represent any rationale save arbitrary standards of convenience. British Columbia prescribes eight jurors, of whom three-quarters may bring in a verdict if the jury is not agreed after three hours. Alberta prescribes six jurors, of whom five may bring in a verdict. The same holds true for Manitoba and for Ontario. In Saskatchewan, the number is still twelve, but a verdict may be brought in by ten. Nova Scotia has settled on nine of whom seven may bring in a verdict if there is no agreement after four hours. Newfoundland prescribes the same numbers, but allows only three hours before unanimity may be abandoned. Prince Edward Island has fixed on a seven-member jury, and five may bring in a verdict if there is no unanimity after one hour's deliberation. New Brunswick prescribes the same numbers of seven and five but provides for a lapse of two hours. Moreover, this Province has a five-member jury in county court actions, of whom four may give a verdict.

As contrasted with the present position in England where civil juries are rare, they are still a flourishing institution in some parts of Canada. Although in some Provinces, for example, Manitoba, the usual mode of trial in civil matters is without a jury, there are nonetheless specified types of action in which a jury is mandatory unless the parties agree to dispense with it. Ontario's jury legislation is similar to that of Manitoba, but jury notices and jury trials abound in Ontario whereas they have almost disappeared in Manitoba. Some recent statistics tell the tale. In absolute terms there were 232 jury trials in Supreme Court actions in Ontario in 1967 and 179 in 1968. In each of those years there were, respectively, close to 900 and 800 actions lodged in which juries were sought, but the vast bulk were settled after being placed on the list for trial. In Manitoba there were no civil cases tried with a jury in 1967 or 1968; in fact, there have been only four civil jury cases in the past twenty-five years and two of them were cases in which such trial was compulsory (because the parties did not agree to dispense with a jury). Applications for jury trial are still made in Manitoba but they represent an empty ritual. In Nova Scotia eight cases were set down for jury trial in 1967 and sixteen in 1968; the number tried by jury was four and eight respectively. The position in Ontario is unique in Canada; the common law disposition to jury trial is evident there in the disinclination to strike out jury notices, especially in running-down cases.

Provision is still made in most of the Provinces for special juries which were in effect abolished in England in 1949. They are very rarely sought; and if any other justification is needed for doing away with special juries, it may be found in the modern legislative and judicial de-emphasis of civil jury trial; the principles on which the courts dispense with ordinary jury trial are no warrant for special juries.

In criminal cases, which are governed by the federal Criminal Code, the old prescription of twelve jurors who must be unanimous still prevails, save that in Alberta and in the Northwest Territories a jury of six is the rule. The Code's direction that every charge of an indictable offence must be tried by a judge and jury is overwhelmed by the qualification "except where otherwise expressly provided by law."[18] Since under the Code a magistrate has absolute jurisdiction in respect of a specified list of offences, similar summary jurisdiction in respect of a large number of offences with the consent of the accused, and, beyond this, the accused has an election in respect of many offences for non-jury trial before a county or district court judge, the number of jury trials of indictable offences is unpredictable save for those few serious offences, such as murder, manslaughter, rape, treason and sedition, and some others where trial by jury is compulsory.

There are, however, statistics of criminal cases tried by jury, prepared by the Dominion Bureau of Statistics, which underline the restricted use and resort to jury trial.[19] I take for illustration the years 1906, 1926, 1946 and 1966, and the following table shows (1) the number of charges of indictable offences throughout Canada in each of those years; (2) the number of cases tried by jury; (3) the percentage of such cases:

[18] Cr. Code, s. 415.

[19] I am indebted to the Dominion Bureau of Statistics and to Mr. Walter E. Duffett, the Dominion Statistician, for supplying this and other information about the incidence of criminal jury trials in Canada.

	(1)	(2)	(3)
1906	10,900	810	7·4
1926	21,976	1,197	5·4
1946	53,959	1,033	1·9
1966	51,080	1,063	2·1

Of course, a more useful breakdown would be to have the number of charges of offences where a jury is compulsory. Information available for 1966 only shows 78 charges of capital and non-capital murder, on which 43 persons were tried (some on more than one such charge), one of whom had his trial without a jury in Alberta under a special Criminal Code provision enabling an accused so to be tried on any indictable offence with his consent; 13 persons so charged were detained for insanity and there was a stay of proceedings in 2 cases. There were 40 charges of attempted murder in the year on which 10 persons were tried (one in Alberta without a jury) and there were 5 detentions for insanity and three cases in which proceedings were stayed. There were 89 charges of manslaughter on which 69 persons were tried, 4 of them in Alberta without a jury. There were 128 charges of rape and 25 of attempted rape on which 63 persons were tried, 13 of them without a jury in Alberta, and there was a stay of proceedings in 12 cases and no bill in 5. It is a safe surmise, when one considers that murder, manslaughter and rape must be tried with a jury, that election of jury trial in other charges of indictable offences is infrequent. In short, the right given in respect of the vast number of offences to elect trial by jury is not being exercised.

I may add here that the Criminal Code gives persons who are arraigned in certain districts in Quebec, where the sheriff is required to return half English-speaking and half

French-speaking jury panels, the right to demand an entirely English- or French-speaking jury if English or French is their language. In Manitoba, an accused whose language is English or French has the right to demand a jury of whom at least half speak his language.

The grand jury, which ceased to exist in England in 1933, is still in existence in Ontario, Nova Scotia, Prince Edward Island and Newfoundland. Its abolition was recommended by the Criminal Code Revision Commission which was responsible for the revised Criminal Code effective April 1, 1955. With trained magistrates conducting preliminary inquiries, and with independent power in the prosecuting authorities to prefer an indictment, the grand jury's role in the criminal process appears to be anachronistic.

THE CONTINUING IMPACT OF ENGLISH LAW

A scanning of Canadian law reports, whether old or current, will amply demonstrate the continuing and pervasive influence of English decisions in Canadian courts. A leading Canadian scholar, writing in 1959 (and there has been no marked change since then), had this to say on the matter [20]:

> " A perusal of Canadian law reports not only verifies an absence of creative approach but conveys the impression that most of the opinions reported there are those of English judges applying English law in Canada, rather than those of Canadian judges develop-

[20] H. E. Read, " The Judicial Process in Common Law Canada " (1959) 37 Can. Bar Rev. 265 at p. 268. The author, a Canadian, was formerly a professor of law at Dalhousie University, then at the University of Minnesota (1934–50) and later Dean of Law at Dalhousie (1950–64).

ing Canadian law to meet Canadian needs with guidance of English precedent."

In the early colonial years, English legal institutions and English legal doctrines were, of course, an obligatory if not also a convenient, starting point. The period during which the colonies evolved to self-government and to responsible government was also a period of considerable reform in English judicial administration, procedure and law; and this helped to give the English tradition a robustness which induced admiration and suggested emulation beyond the compulsion of *stare decisis*. The very vigour of the tradition as it manisfested itself in the 19th century may have had an enervating effect on the Canadian courts, persuading them to accept principles that were ill-adapted to the Canadian condition and from which escape by legislation, especially in respect of private law, was not easily achieved. This, in turn, has produced a dissatisfaction among legal scholars and law teachers in Canada, and they have criticised (to use the words of one of them) "the traditional inarticulate legal positivism of Canadian lawyers and judges." [21]

True it is that prevailing oddities of English law, for example, benefit of clergy, were applied in the early colonial period [22]; and almost the entire stock of feudally inspired principles of real property law, extant in the last half of the 18th century, were likewise fed into the stream of common law decision in Canada. But there were, on

[21] Weiler, "Two Models of Judicial Decision-Making" (1968) 46 Can. Bar Rev. 406.

[22] See Doull, "Benefit of Clergy" (1941) 19 Can. Bar Rev. 22. Examples of resort to benefit of clergy exist in New Brunswick, Nova Scotia and Upper Canada.

the other hand, brave leads given by English judges which deserved ready reception in the colonies. *Somersett's* case in 1772, involving the discharge of a slave on habeas corpus, was echoed in the Quebec courts at the turn of the 19th century, but a contemporary proceeding in New Brunswick failed on an equal division of the court, with Chief Justice Ludlow supporting slavery on the curious ground that he was applying the "common law of the colonies."[23] Later, in Ontario, and long after slavery had been abolished by statute, the court refused to recognise the validity of a marriage of slaves contracted in Virginia in 1825 before a minister but without a licence which, while required, could not be obtained by slaves since they were not regarded as persons under the law of that state.[24] This was not an edifying conclusion.

Manifestations of judicial independence did emerge in the 19th century through the influence of the rigours of frontier life; and where the courts could not be useful allies legislation was invoked. Thus in *Dean* v. *McCarthy*, decided in 1846, an Upper Canada court held that the deliberate setting of a fire to clear land for cultivation did not give rise to absolute liability where the fire spread to adjoining land, and that negligence must be established.[25] The decision was approved later in the face of *Rylands* v. *Fletcher* and long before the exception from it of ordinary or natural user of land was settled.[26]

[23] See Buchanan, *The Bench and Bar of Lower Canada* (1925), pp. 41–42; Lawrence, *The Judges of New Brunswick and Their Times* (1907), p. 71 *et seq.*

[24] *Harris* v. *Cooper* (1870) 31 U.C.Q.B. 182.

[25] (1846) 2 U.C.Q.B.(O.S.) 448.

[26] *Gillson* v. *North Grey Ry.* (1872) 33 U.C.Q.B. 128, affirmed (1874) 35 U.C.Q.B. 475; and see *Fleming on Torts* (3rd ed., 1965), p. 317.

Along the same lines, an Ontario court refused (in its words) to transfer " without discrimination to a new and comparatively unsettled country like this Province all the niceties of the ancient learning as to waste which obtain in England " [27]; and, accordingly, it was held to be lawful for a life tenant to sell timber on the land in order to apply the proceeds to the purchase of suitable lumber to repair buildings; he was not to be limited to the use only of the very timber on the land.

Again, Canadian courts rejected the English distinction between tidal and non-tidal waters as it related to public rights of navigation and to ownership of the bed. A public right of navigation was recognised in navigable waters regardless of ownership of the bed, and the *ad medium filum* rule was applied to non-navigable waters only. Moreover, the needs of the lumbering industry which became so important in the 19th century were met by legislation which carried the right of persons to float their timber down rivers beyond the common law.[28]

Significant as they were for the particular purposes, the departures from English decision were too few to destroy the aptness of the aphorism that they were merely the exceptions that proved the rule. In the field of tort in the 19th century, Canadian courts accepted *Butterfield* v. *Forrester*, barring recovery by a negligent plaintiff, and also the escape from that doctrine through the rule of last clear chance, originating in *Davies* v. *Mann* and ending in the

[27] *Hixon* v. *Reaveley* (1904) 9 O.L.R. 6.

[28] See *Leamy* v. *R.* (1916) 54 S.C.R. 143; *Att.-Gen. Quebec and Hull* v. *Scott* (1904) 34 S.C.R. 603; *Fort George Lumber Co.* v. *Grand Trunk Pacific Ry.* (1915) 9 W.W.R. 17. See, for example, Rivers and Streams Act, R.S.O. 1897, c. 142.

sophistication of *British Columbia Electric Railway Ltd.* v. *Loach.* Even the Quebec courts accepted the common law rule on the effect of contributory negligence until, following the promulgation of the Quebec Civil Code in 1866, the principle of *faute commune* and resulting apportionment took over. Apportionment legislation, bearing within it the basis for the virtual disappearance of the last clear chance principle, now prevails in the common law Provinces.[29]

In the law of master and servant, the disabling doctrine of common employment of *Priestley* v. *Fowler* was accepted in the common law Provinces until swept away by workmen's compensation legislation.[30] This social insurance scheme, pioneered by Ontario, also did away with contributory negligence and voluntary assumption of risk as bars to compensation for injury suffered in the course of employment. English decisions were closely followed in the working out of vicarious tort liability, in the development of the law on damages in both contract and tort, and, indeed, in the substantive principles of liability in those branches of the law. The list of acknowledgments, were I to extend them, would be almost endless.

Perhaps as great a testament of faith in English decisions as can be found in Canada is the respect accorded to *Indermaur* v. *Dames* and the progeny it has spawned in the law of occupiers' liability. It is not too much to say that the words of Willes J. in that case have been raised to the

[29] The matter is fully discussed by MacIntyre, "The Rationale of Last Clear Chance" (1940) 18 Can. Bar Rev. 665, and in "Last Clear Chance after Thirty Years" (1955) 33 Can. Bar Rev. 257.

[30] See, for example, *Root* v. *Vancouver Power Co.* (1912) 2 D.L.R. 303. The pioneer Ontario measure was enacted by 1914 (Ont.), c. 25. The doctrine of common employment survived in England until the Law Reform (Common Employment) Act 1951.

level of statute, each phrase carefully examined and the entire relevant passage regarded as comprehensively embodying almost eternal principle. The enactment of the Occupiers' Liability Act 1957 in the United Kingdom has so far had no response here, either in legislation or in judicial decision; our courts do not appear to favour Pound's proposition that legislation no less than decided cases elsewhere may provide fresh starting points for reconsideration of old authorities. Thus, for example, *London Graving Dock Co. Ltd.* v. *Horton*, much condemned by scholarly writing in Canada, continues to be accepted by the courts although it was expressly overturned by the Act of 1957 in so far as it held that an invitee's knowledge of the dangerous condition of premises relieves the occupier of his duty of care.[31]

Another area of faithful adherence has been the law of landlord and tenant, with the property philosophy triumphing over the contractual as in England. But what is worse, there has been no such legislative response in Canada to the imbalance of the judicial law of landlord and tenant as there has been in England. It is only recently that the prospect has opened up in Ontario, thanks to its Law Reform Commission, of bringing that law into the 20th century.[32] The English common law and equitable doctrines in that branch of the law not only took their inspiration from the notion of the "estate," notwithstanding the fact that a leasehold was categorised as personalty, but in the spilling over of the estate principle into the consideration of the lease covenants (as, for example, the lessee's covenant

[31] [1951] A.C. 737; and for criticism, see Harris, Note (1964) 42 Can. Bar Rev. 607; Wright, *Cases on the Law of Torts* (4th ed., 1967), pp. 666–668, 754–757.

[32] See its recent Interim Report on Landlord and Tenant Law Applicable to Residential Tenancies (1968).

to repair) the law developed around the long-term English residential lease which never became prevalent in Canada.

On real property law proper, our record of reform has been dismal compared to that of the United Kingdom. We aped the statutory reforms in the English law to the turn of the century and then stopped. There has been a resurgence of interest in real property reform in the last few years, again owing to the lead of the Ontario Law Reform Commission. The first fruit of its labours, after its establishment in the early part of 1964, was a draft Perpetuities Act, embodying the "wait and see" rule, which was enacted into law in 1966.[33] It is as well a monument to the late Dean Wright, the most penetrating scholarly expositor and critic of the law that Canada has produced; it was on his report and his draft statute that the Commission relied in recommending legislative action to the Government.

Of course, there has been a good deal of legislation affecting real property relations that has outflanked the common law and even some of its statutory modifications.[34] Registry Acts, Land Titles Acts, planning legislation, oil and gas legislation in the western Provinces and, more recently, condominium legislation have reduced the effect of the heritage of feudal rules[35]; but residual pockets of anachronisms remain, as pitfalls for the unwary who today are usually those who insist on drawing their own wills or

[33] 1966 (Ont.), c. 113. The wide acceptance of the rule is commented on by Lang in (1962) 40 Can. Bar Rev. 294.

[34] For example, British Columbia abolished the rule in *Whitby* v. *Mitchell* (1890) 44 Ch.D. 85 by 1957 (B.C.), c. 33, s. 2; it disappeared in England under its 1925 property legislation but still obtains in Ontario.

[35] See, for example, the Condominium Act 1967 (Ont.), c. 12; and see Risk, "Condominiums and Canada" (1968) 18 U. of T.L.J. 1; Sinclair, "Condominium in Canada" (1968) 46 Can. Bar Rev. 1.

drafting their own agreements. Since in the law of property the courts have, understandably, favoured stability and have acted on the footing that decisions on property transactions should rarely be disturbed, redemption must be sought from the legislature.

Two other areas in which the English judicial example has been whole-heartedly followed (and which deserve more than the brief mention I accord them here) are statutory interpretation and judicial review of the decisions of administrative tribunals. The severe limitations on resort to extrinsic materials have been carried over to constitutional interpretation where their rationale of exclusion seems to me to be indefensible. In the field of judicial review, even making allowance for the technical procedural problems which the prerogative writs raise (depending on how the courts see fit to treat them), the norms of review give more evidence of their hierarchical origins of securing conformity to curial standards than of concern to permit independent tribunals to develop their own and perhaps different standards. This is particularly the case in matters which have become justiciable for the first time under the legislative regime which has given life to the independent tribunal; the prime illustration in Canada is the labour relations field with its labour relations boards and its labour-management arbitration boards. The avidity with which Canadian courts embraced *R.* v. *Northumberland Compensation Appeal Tribunal, ex p. Shaw* and applied it in the labour relations field is testimony not only to the erudition of the judgment but to its utility in providing another control lever in respect of administrative adjudications.[36]

[36] [1952] 1 K.B. 338; applied by the Supreme Court of Canada in *Board of Industrial Relations (Alta.) et al.* v. *Stedelbauer Chevrolet Oldsmobile*

Two other observations are in order on the hospitality with which English decisions are received in Canada. A good deal of legislation in the common law Provinces and a good deal of federal legislation has been taken, in more or less literal appropriation, from the United Kingdom Statute Book; and, inevitably, the *in pari materia* approach to statutory construction has brought English cases into play on the interpretation of Canadian statutes. Second, English judgments have exhibited (and continue to do so) a literary flavour and a lucidity which have reinforced the persuasiveness of the propositions of law which they embodied. They have, accordingly, tempted quotation by Canadian courts, at times to the point where their judgments exemplified what Cardozo called the tonsorial or agglutinative method of formulation.

Withal, Canadian judicial creativity has not run dry even if one could wish for less obvious dependency on the judicial work of another jurisdiction.[37] Mr. Justice Riddell twice, more than a quarter of a century ago, introduced the notion of warranty as a basis for the liability of a producer of defective food products to a consumer.[38] Its implications were worked through in the United States to a principle of strict liability, but it has remained an unanswered call in Canada. In *Fleming* v. *Atkinson* in 1959 the Supreme Court of Canada refused to accept the House of Lords judgment

Ltd. (1968) 1 D.L.R. (3d) 81; and see also *Re Newhall and Reimer* (1968) 2 D.L.R. (3d) 498.

37 Read, *op. cit.*, note 20, gives a number of examples in his excellent article.

38 *Shandloff* v. *City Dairy* [1936] O.R. 579; *Arendale* v. *Canada Bread Co. Ltd.* [1941] 2 D.L.R. 41. See the discussion by Linden, "Products Liability in Canada," in Linden (ed.), *Studies in Canadian Tort Law* (1968), p. 216 *et seq.*

in *Searle* v. *Wallbank* as stating the common law of Ontario, and imposed liability, under the ordinary principles of negligence, upon an owner of cattle straying on the highway for injury to a passing motorist.[39]

Nor has English judicial creativity or leadership always found ready acceptance in Canada. The Supreme Court of Canada rejected "the joint assets" doctrine in matrimonial cases as it developed in a line of English Court of Appeal decisions, refusing to find any basis for it in the discretionary power vested in the court under the Married Women's Property Act. Its judgment, moreover, seemed to point as well to a probable denial of any interest in a deserted wife in the matrimonial home. The principle, which had been accepted in the provincial courts, had not at that time been demolished by the House of Lords, only to be restored by legislation.[40] Again, the Ontario Court of Appeal preferred to follow its own course on the applicable principles to govern the award of exemplary damages rather than to follow the House of Lords in *Rookes* v. *Barnard*.[41]

I offer one other illustration. In *R.* v. *Snider*, the Supreme Court of Canada, concerned though it was with Crown privilege from production in a criminal rather than

[39] [1959] S.C.R. 513.

[40] [1961] S.C.R. 3. Acceptance of the English law on the interest of a deserted wife in the matrimonial home is seen in *Re Jollow and Jollow* [1955] 1 D.L.R. 601. When the House of Lords rejected the doctrine, a Canadian court followed suit: see *Stevens* v. *Brown* (1969) 2 D.L.R. (3d) 687. The House of Lords judgment is *National Provincial Bank Ltd.* v. *Ainsworth* [1965] A.C. 1175, reversed by the Matrimonial Homes Act 1967 (U.K.), c. 75.

[41] See *Gouzenko* v. *Lefolii* [1967] 2 O.R. 262, affirmed on other grounds (1968) 70 D.L.R. (2d) 337. For an Australian disavowal, see *Uren* v. *John Fairfax & Sons Pty. Ltd.* [1967] A.L.R. 25.

in a civil proceeding, took a view of the matter that differed from the executive-minded approach in *Duncan* v. *Cammell Laird & Co.*; its judgment was rather consonant with the later decision in *Conway* v. *Rimmer* which provided an early test of the House of Lords proclamation of freedom to depart from its previous decisions.[42]

What I have said about common law Canada has but limited application to Quebec where a Civil Code prevails both in respect of substantive law and of procedure. But the English influence is not negligible. The impact of English law, about which some writers in Quebec have expressed concern,[43] is long standing and did not begin with Canadian federalism. It is seen in the conduct of trials[44]; in the fact that English rules of evidence in commercial matters were adopted in 1785 and later extended in 1847 in accordance with an earlier extension in England under Lord Tenterden's Act in 1828; in the fact that commercial law itself has English as well as French components[45]; and in the fact that English supervisory remedies, the prerogative writs and habeas corpus, are part of the legal structure of Quebec. There is even, in Quebec, an institution, the *fiducie*, which is not unlike the trust of English law and hence quite alien to the French law which does not recognise the English distinction between legal and equitable ownership.[46]

42 The respective judgments are reported in [1954] S.C.R. 479, [1942] A.C. 624 and [1968] A.C. 910.

43 See Morin, "L'Anglicisation de notre droit civil" (1937) 40 Rev. du Not. 145.

44 See Watt, "The Trial of Civil Cases in Quebec" [1960] R.L. 65.

45 See W. S. Johnson, "Sources of the Quebec Law of Evidence in Civil and Commercial Matters" (1953) 31 Can. Bar Rev. 1000.

46 Civil Code, art. 981a *et seq.*, introduced by 1879 (Que.), c. 29; *Curran* v. *Davis* [1933] S.C.R. 283.

English Decisions And Stare Decisis in Canadian Courts

Long before there was any well understood or articulated doctrine of *stare decisis* respecting the binding effect of at least House of Lords decisions in Canadian courts, English judgments were followed or applied simply because they represented the source of the common law received in the colonies. The opinions of the Privy Council were, of course, binding under the classical rule of *stare decisis*; but an Ontario judge applied the qualification that only its decisions in Canadian appeals were compelling and not those given in appeals to it from other jurisdictions.[47] The qualification was never endorsed by either the Supreme Court of Canada or by the Privy Council.

The Privy Council's pre-eminent position in the Canadian judicial structure, although not *per se* complicating, did raise difficulties following its pronouncements in (1) *Trimble* v. *Hill* in 1879 that a colonial court should follow the English Court of Appeal (where the House of Lords has not given a contrary decision) on the construction of like enactments[48]; and (2) *Robins* v. *National Trust Co. Ltd.* in 1927 that a colony "regulated" or "bound" by English law is bound to follow the House of Lords where it has settled the law (as well as being bound by the Privy Council), but it is not to be assumed that a colonial appellate court is wrong if it differs from an English appellate court (other than the House of Lords).[49] Canadian courts threshed about

[47] *Negro* v. *Pietro's Bread Co.* [1933] O.R. 112; criticised by Marshall, "The Binding Effect of Decisions of the Judicial Committee of the Privy Council" (1968) 17 I.C.L.Q. 743.

[48] (1879) 5 App.Cas. 342.

[49] [1927] A.C. 515.

with *Trimble* v. *Hill*, some reading it broadly, some narrowly; but it is fair to say that even before Privy Council appeals were abolished *Trimble* v. *Hill* was very narrowly applied, if at all, by reason of any principle of *stare decisis*.[50] Rather English Court of Appeal decisions were accepted and applied without any consciousness of obligation but because they reflected agreeable propositions of law. In the end result, however, deference did not differ very much from duty.

One cannot be certain that *Trimble* v. *Hill* was intended to apply to the Supreme Court of Canada; it was, after all, an appeal from the Supreme Court of New South Wales. The Supreme Court of Canada had, however, already been established a few years at the time of *Trimble* v. *Hill*, and in its own decisions it seemed to recognise the authority of the English Court of Appeal, a posture that ceased to be necessary, if it ever was, after *Robins* v. *National Trust Co. Ltd.*

The *Robins* doctrine suggested that if there was a difference between the House of Lords and the Privy Council, the former should be followed by a Canadian court; and this did happen.[51] But the problem also arose whether a provincial court should follow the Supreme Court of Canada or the House of Lords where the Privy Council had not taken a position; and in one case at least the decision of the Supreme Court of Canada was preferred.[52] The Privy Council itself has recently affirmed the right of

50 See the discussion in Hodgins, " The Authority of English Decisions " (1923) 1 Can. Bar Rev. 470.

51 See *Will* v. *Bank of Montreal* [1931] 3 D.L.R. 526.

52 See *Georgia Construction Co.* v. *Pacific Great Eastern Ry.* [1929] 1 D.L.R. 77.

the High Court of Australia to differ from the House of Lords on what is certainly a point of English law, namely, the situations in which exemplary damages may be awarded [53]; and although this may merely reflect the respect in which the High Court of Australia is held, it also suggests the end of the hegemony of the English version of the common law, of which other warnings have been given by the High Court of Australia itself. That court had a little earlier declared its independence of the House of Lords and its right to formulate its own views unhampered by House of Lords decisions.[54]

The abolition of Privy Council appeals has, of course, on any rational assessment of Canada's position (taking into consideration as well the Statute of Westminster) freed Canadian courts of any obligation to respect English decisions, whatever be their level, except as a matter of their merit. Even so, there have been some cases in which Canadian judges have either forgotten or preferred to ignore their statutory liberation.[55] When the abolition measure was pending there was considerable discussion—how barren it looks today—about the continuing force of past Privy Council decisions and a proposal that the Supreme Court of Canada adopt the Privy Council's then one-judgment rule. The first of these matters was left to the Supreme Court of Canada to deal with; and it has done so, sensibly asserting its right to act as freely as the Privy Council itself

[53] *Australian Consolidated Press Ltd.* v. *Uren* [1967] 3 All E.R. 523.
[54] *Cf. Parker* v. *R.* (1963) 37 Aust.L.J.R. 3 at p. 11; *Skelton* v. *Collins* (1966) 39 Aust.L.J.R. 480.
[55] See, for example, *Re Cox* [1950] 2 D.L.R. 449 at p. 468, reversed on other grounds [1951] O.R. 205, affirmed [1953] 1 S.C.R. 94, affirmed [1955] A.C. 627; *Power* v. *Stoyles* (1958) 17 D.L.R. (2d) 239.

could.[56] The second was not adopted; and it did not need the hindsight of the Privy Council's own rejection of the one-judgment rule to certify to the bankruptcy of such a proposal for a final court in a federal system.

Stare decisis is now an internal matter for Canadian courts, both as it relates to the provincial appellate courts individually and as it relates to the Supreme Court's view of its own decisions and its responsibility as a branch of government. There are companion issues of judicial comity as between judges of co-ordinate jurisdiction within the same hierarchy, as between judges of different provincial courts of first instance, and as between judges of provincial and federal courts, and as between the different provincial appellate courts; and these are no less matters of self-determination than is *stare decisis*, subject only to the ukase of a higher governing court. Some of the explanations given in the cases to explain why judicial comity is extended do not differ in substance from the various considerations which the English Court of Appeal set out in *Young* v. *Bristol Aeroplane Co. Ltd.* as permitting it to depart from its previous decisions.[57] It is also pertinent to observe that it is one thing to extend judicial comity by acquiescing in the construction of a contract or a statute or in the determination of factual issues which were before another court (and when neither *stare decisis* nor *res judicata* applies), and it is quite a different thing to accept as a matter of judicial comity principles of law enunciated by another

[56] See *Reference re Ontario Farm Products Marketing Act* [1957] S.C.R. 198 at p. 212; *Binus* v. *R.* [1967] S.C.R. 594 at p. 601; *Drew* v. *R.* [1961] S.C.R. 614.

[57] For an illustration of comity as between a provincial court and the Exchequer Court of Canada, see *John Bertram & Sons Ltd.* v. *R.* [1968] 2 Ex.C.R. 590. *Young* v. *Bristol Aeroplane Co. Ltd.* is reported in [1944] K.B. 718.

court. It is difficult to see why comity should be invoked in the latter case if the court before which the question of comity arises does not agree with the enunciation. Where, however, federal legislation or similar legislation in the Provinces has been construed and applied, comity is a way of expressing the virtue of uniformity.[58]

The Supreme Court of Canada has never instructed provincial appellate courts to follow their own decisions, and *stare decisis* practice has varied among the provincial appellate courts.[59] The Ontario Court of Appeal, of all such courts, has been the most consistently self-limiting in respect of its previous decisions; and has recently refused (albeit by a majority only) to agree that it could depart from a previous decision even in a criminal case, thereby adopting a position more rigid than that of the English Court of Appeal.[60] The latter's recent majority reaffirmation of *stare decisis* in civil cases in *Gallie* v. *Lee*, despite the example of the House of Lords in removing its previously self-imposed fetters, is, to say the least, surprising.[61]

One peculiarly Canadian problem respecting *stare decisis* concerns the authority of Supreme Court of Canada

[58] See, for example, *Re Vinarao* (1968) 66 D.L.R. (2d) 736 at p. 739.

[59] See MacGuigan, " Precedent and Policy in the Supreme Court " (1967) 45 Can. Bar Rev. 627 at p. 652 *et seq*. Friedmann, " *Stare Decisis* at Common Law and under the Civil Code of Quebec " (1953) 31 Can. Bar Rev. 722.

[60] *R*. v. *De Clercq* [1966] 1 O.R. 674, affirmed on other grounds [1968] S.C.R. 902. On the civil side, see *London Assurance Co*. v. *Jonassen* (1968) 66 D.L.R. (2d) 692 at p. 695.

[61] [1969] 1 All E.R. 1062. The writer of the Note in (1968) 84 L.Q.R. 299 who said that " the [English] Court of Appeal now is the only appellate court in the whole world which clings to a precedent merely because it is a precedent . . . [and] it represents a system that has died out elsewhere " flatters some at least of the Canadian provincial appellate courts and certainly the Ontario Court of Appeal.

decisions in Quebec, and especially when those decisions concern Civil Code principles. The civil law tradition is, as has been said elsewhere, to decide " by the authority of reason rather than by reason of authority "; and the Quebec Court of Appeal has given evidence of its adherence to this view, not only with respect to its own decisions, but in some cases even with respect to judgments of the Supreme Court of Canada.[62] On the other hand, the Supreme Court of Canada has said that it is at the summit for Quebec as for other Provinces, and that the rule of obedience of lower courts to higher courts in the hierarchy applies in respect of cases from Quebec as from elsewhere in Canada.[63] Quebec courts will necessarily have to accept this position and must look for extrication to a loosening by the Supreme Court of its own attitude of adherence to its previous decisions.

The central question in *stare decisis* is, however, not so much the danger of constantly shifting legal principles if the doctrine is abandoned—the judicial function is not an undisciplined one—but rather the role and, indeed, the utility of dissenting opinions. It can, of course, be said that a dissent may be useful to a higher court called upon to consider the particular question or to support a legislative

62 See Anglin, *Stare Decisis and Other Subjects as Viewed in the Civil Law and at Common Law* (1922), p. 23; see *Lavallee* v. *Bellefleur* [1958] Que.Q.B. 53 at p. 58; *Lemay* v. *Dufresne* (1908) 18 Que.K.B. 132, refusing to follow *Meloche* v. *Simpson* (1899) 29 S.C.R. 375; a series of such refusals followed, but ultimately the Quebec Court of Appeal had to recognise the binding effect of Supreme Court of Canada decisions: see *Lavallee* v. *Bellefleur* [1958] Que.Q.B. 53; and see Mignault, " The Authority of Decided Cases " (1925) 3 Can. Bar Rev. 1.

63 See *Salvas* v. *Vassal* (1896) 27 S.C.R. 68 at p. 89; *Daoust Lalonde & Cie Ltee.* v. *Ferland* [1932] S.C.R. 343 at p. 351, applying *stare decisis* to the Supreme Court itself in respect of appeals from Quebec.

remedy. These are not convincing reconciliations of dissenting opinions with the maintenance of *stare decisis*, especially where constitutional questions are involved. And, in the face of *stare decisis*, is persistence in dissent permissible? "Holmes and Brandeis JJ. dissenting" had meaning in a final court which had no illusions about eternal verities or the long-term value of stability for stability's sake. Experience with this issue in the Supreme Court of Canada shows that dissent has no survival value if *stare decisis* is the rule.[64]

It seems to me that Cardozo put the whole problem in perspective in three short sentences, as follows: "All agree that there may be dissent when the opinion is filed. Some would seem to hold that there must be none a moment thereafter. Plenary inspiration has then descended upon the work of the majority."[65] The rebuke is gentle, and the appeal is to act grown-up.

The Supreme Court of Canada has, recently, abandoned in word (but cautious word) and in covert deed its now three-score-year-old acceptance of *stare decisis* in respect of its own decisions.[66] It has said, plainly enough, that it can depart from its previous decisions; the lately deceased former Justice Rand, one of the most illustrious members that the court has had, said earlier that it could depart from Privy Council decisions; and it is my analysis of a number

[64] For example, Cartwright J., who dissented in *O'Grady* v. *Sparling* [1960] S.C.R. 804, delivered the majority judgment of the court in *Mann* v. *R.* [1966] S.C.R. 238 which rested, in part at least, on *O'Grady* v. *Sparling*; see also *R.* v. *George* [1966] S.C.R. 267; *R.* v. *Sikyea* [1964] S.C.R. 642 and *Daniels* v. *R.* (1968) 2 D.L.R. (3d) 1 at p. 4.

[65] *The Nature of the Judicial Process* (1921), p. 29.

[66] As laid down in *Stuart* v. *Bank of Montreal* (1909) 41 S.C.R. 516.

of Supreme Court of Canada decisions that it has done both of these things, but without the blare of trumpets.[67]

That must come to round out the Supreme Court's position as a final court. All ultimate courts have had to endure the jingle that they are not final because they are infallible; they are infallible because they are final. The Supreme Court will not be any less final because it is confessedly fallible. What has been troubling about it—and this may be partly the consequence of having been for a long time a captive court and partly the consequence of its adherence to *stare decisis*—is its frequent concern to find authority for propositions of law that are put in issue before it.[68] A. P. Herbert had one of his fictional judges remark that "there is no precedent for anything until it is done for the first time."[69] The Supreme Court is uniquely the court to which other Canadian courts must look to create a precedent rather than the court which must itself seek one.

[67] See, for example, *Att.-Gen. Ont.* v. *Barfried Enterprises Ltd.* [1963] S.C.R. 570; and *cf.* with *Reference re Section 6 of the Saskatchewan Farm Security Act 1944* [1947] S.C.R. 394, affirmed [1949] A.C. 110; *Peda* v. *R.* (1969), judgment of Supreme Court, June 2, as yet unreported; and *cf.* with *Binus* v. *R.* [1967] S.C.R. 594.

[68] See *Frey* v. *Fedoruk* [1950] S.C.R. 517 at p. 525; *cf. Brewer* v. *McCauley* [1954] S.C.R. 645 at p. 649; and see criticism by Kennedy, Note (1955) 33 Can. Bar Rev. 340; *National Trust Co. Ltd.* v. *Wong Aviation Co. Ltd.* (1969) 3 D.L.R. (3d) 55 at p. 62.

[69] *Uncommon Law* (1936), p. 109.

3

BALANCING CONSIDERATIONS: LAW REPORTS, LEGAL EDUCATION AND LEGAL SCHOLARSHIP IN CANADA

THE young Canadian colonies, with newly established courts and very small Bars, had to wait some years before local legal materials became available to assist in the administration of justice; in the meantime they had to rely on English books, statutes and reports and on similar materials from the American states. An appreciation of the limited resources in the early years can be gleaned from the first catalogue, published in 1829, of the holdings of the library of the Law Society of Upper Canada which was established in 1827. It listed 264 volumes, mostly English nominate reports but including Brooke's *Abridgment*, Coke's *Institutes*, the *Code Napoleon*, Fitzherbert's *Abridgment*, Hawkins' *Pleas of the Crown*, *Pothier on Obligations*, Rolle's *Abridgment*, Sheppard's *Touchstone*, Viner's *Abridgment* and the *Year Books*. The only local volume was Taylor's *Reports of King's Bench Cases in Upper Canada*, covering the years 1823 to 1827. Surprisingly, Blackstone's *Commentaries* does not appear, and there are no American materials listed.

It took time to put even the printing of statutes and ordinances on a regular publication basis. Thus, the ordinances establishing civil government in Quebec, in 1764 and following years, were first printed for the years 1764 to 1767 in the latter year. The first statutes of Upper Canada, enacted in 1792, were not printed for public use until 1795 (along with the laws to that date), although the enactments of 1793 were printed separately in that earlier year, apparently because the printer started in business at that time. Chief Justice Belcher provided the first compilation of the laws of Nova Scotia in 1767, and revisions of "perpetual" and "temporary" Acts of the Province also appeared in that year. All Canadian Provinces and the central Government now follow the practice of periodic consolidation and revision of their statutes, collecting the annual output since the latest revision, and consolidating the whole to provide in convenient form easier and at the same time contemporary citation.

Canadian law reporting had a much later start.[1] Contemporary reporting of cases was unknown until after the first quarter of the 19th century, save for a one volume collection of cases in the Court of King's Bench for the Quebec District of Lower Canada, decided in 1809 and 1810, collected and edited by George Pyke and published in 1811. Pyke, a member of the Bar of Nova Scotia (where he was born) and later of the Bar of Lower Canada, became Attorney-General of Lower Canada in 1812 and subsequently a judge of its Court of King's Bench.

In 1823, a statute of Upper Canada provided for the appointment by the Government of a member of the Law Society of Upper Canada as reporter of decisions of the Court of King's Bench. He was to be an officer of the court and was to submit a fair report of decisions to the judges for their signature, thereby making them an "authentic

1 See the references in Brown, P. A. Maxwell and L. F. Maxwell, *A Legal Bibliography of the British Commonwealth of Nations* (1957), Vol. 3.

report of all such decisions." [2] Taylor, already mentioned, who was a Bencher of the Law Society, was the first reporter; his successor William Henry Draper, later a Chief Justice of the Province, published a volume of cases for the years 1829 to 1831. This official reporter system was abandoned in 1840 and replaced by statutory provision for appointment of a Queen's Bench reporter by the Law Society. In 1845, the Law Society was empowered to appoint a reporter for Chancery cases; and when the Court of Common Pleas was established in 1849, a reporter of cases in that court was also appointed by the Society. From the very beginning of law reporting in Upper Canada a fee was levied on members of the Bar to support the reporter's salary; and the cost of the annual practising certificate still reflects a sum for subscription to the *Ontario Reports*. The Law Society of Upper Canada is now the only such body in common law Canada that publishes law reports. There is no competing series of reports of Ontario cases only; commercial publishers either include Ontario cases in such special collections as bankruptcy reports, insurance reports and tax cases or include them comprehensively in the Canada-wide general series known as the *Dominion Law Reports*.

New Brunswick, like Upper Canada, provided for a government-appointed reporter, doing this in 1836 after Judge Ward Chipman had collected and annotated cases decided between 1825 and 1835.[3] Nova Scotia followed

[2] 1823 (U.C.), c. 3. The history of early law reporting in Upper Canada is recounted in Riddell, *The Legal Profession in Upper Canada* (1916), cc. 19 and 20.

[3] 1836 (N.B.), c. 14. This Act was of limited duration but was extended from time to time and survives in substance in the Judicature Act, R.S.N.B. 1952, c. 120, ss. 62 (am. 1960, c. 43, s. 3) and 63.

suit in 1845, but its "official" reporter awaited financial support from the legislature which did not come until 1853.[4] In the meantime another barrister collected and published in 1853 various judgments of Chief Justice Halliburton delivered between 1834 and 1851. Both in New Brunswick and Nova Scotia (as in Upper Canada), the early volumes spanned a number of years but annual volumes appeared in time and the system lasted in both Provinces until 1929.

In that year a series organised by a commercial publisher and known as the *Maritime Province Reports* was begun, covering Prince Edward Island as well as New Brunswick and Nova Scotia, and, eventually, Newfoundland after it became a Province in 1949. The *Maritime Province Reports* ceased publication after the 53rd volume was published for 1967–68. The field it covered has been left to the *Dominion Law Reports* (which began in 1912), subject, however, to the reporting of New Brunswick cases in a new series of reports for that Province alone, which was inaugurated at the beginning of 1969 with the approval of the Barristers' Society of the Province. Although otherwise national in scope the *Dominion Law Reports* embrace but a limited number of Quebec cases; unless they have been appealed to the Supreme Court of Canada or are decisions of Quebec courts of general interest to common law lawyers, they are not likely to be published in this series.

Law reporting in Prince Edward Island and Newfoundland has been sporadic because there has not been very much to report. In the former, three volumes collect cases between 1850 and 1882; and an abandoned series, the *Eastern Law Reporter*, embraced cases (including also those from New

[4] See the preface to 2 N.S.R. (James).

Brunswick and Nova Scotia) between 1906 and 1914; and in the latter, after two early collections, each in one volume, covering the period 1817 to 1828, the Law Society of Newfoundland assumed responsibility and saw to the periodic publication of reports to 1946. Since the cessation of the *Maritime Province Reports*, both Prince Edward Island and Newfoundland look to the *Dominion Law Reports* alone for publication of cases from their courts.

Law reporting in Quebec was not regularised until 1892 when the organised Bar began the publication of two series of official reports, one of decisions of the Court of Queen's Bench; and the other of decisions of the Superior Court; a third series of *Quebec Practice Reports* was begun in 1897.[5] All three series have continued and have displaced earlier series which themselves carried on where a number of older unrelated series of reports stopped. Except for short breaks, there is now a record of judicial decisions in Quebec, beginning in 1663 with the French régime and carrying through the British take-over and to the date when the current official reports were begun.

The four western Provinces followed the later example of Upper Canada or Ontario in that in each of them the Law Society undertook the reporting and publication of the decisions of the courts as collected and judged worthy of publication by appointed editors. Each of these series was abandoned by the particular Law Society, and the required service left to be supplied by commercial publishers. The *British Columbia Reports* ended in 1947, after covering the period from 1867 on; the *Alberta Law Reports* took in cases from 1907 to 1932; the *Saskatchewan*

[5] See now the Bar Act 1966–67 (Que.), c. 77, s. 13 (1) (*b*).

Law Reports covered the period 1907 to 1931; and the *Manitoba Reports* covered the period 1883 to 1963, there being also earlier volumes by nominate reporters. Competing with them from 1905 to 1916 was the *Western Law Reporter*; and, from 1912, both the *Western Weekly Reports*, an all-western series, and the *Dominion Law Reports*.

A variety of reports of cases dealing with particular areas of the law have appeared and disappeared over the years. Apart from a few special series which still carry on as business ventures,[6] and apart from the *Supreme Court of Canada Reports* and the *Exchequer Court of Canada Reports*, the general reporting of cases in the common law Provinces is now in the hands of the two commercial publishers of the *Western Weekly Reports* and the *Dominion Law Reports*. Each has also a Canada-wide criminal law report series which regularly includes decisions from all courts, however inferior or superior, as contrasted with the practice of the *Western Weekly Reports* and the *Dominion Law Reports* to concentrate on the decisions of the superior courts and the appellate courts including those of the Supreme Court of Canada.

The Supreme Court and Exchequer Court Reports stand as unique operations in Canadian law reporting because each issues, so to speak, from the court itself under the direction of the Registrar.[7] However, this does not give the reports any special advantage as authoritative embodiments

6 For example, the *Insurance Law Reporter*; the *Canadian Patent Reporter*; the *Canadian Bankruptcy Reports*; *Canadian Railway and Transport Cases*; *Canada Tax Cases*; *Canada Tax Appeal Board Cases*; *Dominion Tax Cases*.

7 Supreme Court Act, R.S.C. 1952, c. 259, s. 18; there is no express authority in the Exchequer Court Act, R.S.C. 1952, c. 98, for publication of reports.

of judicial decisions because the judgments are available to anyone who pays the stamp fee; and although there may be Crown copyright in the courts' reasons, it is unthinkable that it should be asserted to prevent any private person from publishing them in a report series. The judgments have the character of public documents and there is great appeal in the American rule that no one has an exclusive right to publish the laws of a country.[8] The fact, therefore, that judgments of the Supreme Court have an official publication source should not mean that when published in a commercial publisher's series they are less valid as authorities than other decisions of the court published only in the "official" series. In *R.* v. *Reners* in the Alberta Appellate Division, Chief Justice Harvey, faced with the conflicting decisions of the English Court of Appeal in *Lyons* v. *Wilkins* and *Ward, Lock & Co.* v. *Operative Printers' Assistants Society* chose to follow the former for reasons which included a questioning of the *Ward, Lock* decision because it was not reported "in the regularly authorised series of reports" but only in *The Times Law Reports.*[9] I do not think that this is a "choice of law" principle that has anything to commend it.

Legal Education in Canada: Admission to Practice

Writing near the close of the 19th century, the editor of a leading Canadian legal journal, E. D. Armour, who was a law lecturer and a respected author in the field of property,

[8] See Fox, *The Canadian Law of Copyright and Industrial Design* (2nd ed., 1967) at p. 269; Fox, "Copyright in relation to the Crown and Universities" (1947) 7 U. of T.L.J. 98 at p. 115.

[9] [1926] 1 W.W.R. 810 at p. 812, affirmed without reference to this point [1926] S.C.R. 499.

remarked that "unfortunately there are few men in Canada who devote much time to the abstract study of the law, and there is very little encouragement for those who do."[10] A few years earlier, the then President of the Royal Society of Canada, not a lawyer but an historian who wrote widely on Canadian constitutionalism, noted in his presidential address in 1893 on "Canada's Intellectual Strength and Weakness" that the law was becoming more of a technical and less of a learned profession. "Several excellent books of a purely technical character have been compiled from year to year," he said, "but no Kent or Story or Cooley has yet appeared to instruct us by a luminous exposition of principle or breadth of knowledge."[11] Books of the comprehensive character of those written by Kent, Story and Cooley have still not appeared in Canada, but the reference itself to three American scholars at least represented a yearning. The prospects for satisfying it are now better than they have ever been.

If there is anything unique today in Canadian legal education, it is in the understandings—perhaps alliances is as apt—between the integrated Bar (represented in each Province by a Law Society) and university law schools, for both a separation and co-ordination of functions in preparing persons for admission to the practice of law. The system is different from that prevailing in England, where the conditions of qualification are complicated by the existence of separate governing bodies for barristers and solicitors; and different from that in the United States where there is no integrated Bar control of education for law or of

[10] (1899) 19 C.L.T. 309.

[11] J. G. Bourinot in Royal Society of Canada Series § 1 (1893).

eligibility to practise law. The prevailing Canadian scheme of full-time academic study in independent law schools and then a consecutive period of apprenticeship and in some cases also organised clinical training is the culmination of more than a century's development.

The first mention of lawyers in the ordinances that followed upon the establishment by Britain of civil government in Quebec is in the ordinance of September 17, 1764. After providing for a Court of Common Pleas, the so-called court for French-speaking Canadians, it said simply that "Canadian advocates, proctors, etc., may practise in this Court." A succeeding ordinance of July 1, 1766, enlarged this permission by stating that Canadian barristers, advocates, attorneys and proctors may practise in all or any of the courts of the Province (thus including the Court of King's Bench) "under such regulations as shall be prescribed by the said Courts respectively for persons in general under those descriptions." No educational or other formal qualifications for practice were imposed until an ordinance of 1785, the same one that prohibited a barrister or an attorney from being at the same time a notary, and vice versa. It appears that until 1785, the right to practise depended upon a licence from the Governor. The ordinance of 1785 required a five-year indentureship with a qualified advocate or attorney practising in the Province or in some other part of His Majesty's Dominions or six years' service with some clerk or registrar of a Court of Common Pleas or Court of Appeals in the Province, subject to an exception in favour of those called to the Bar or admitted to practise as advocate or attorney in a court of civil jurisdiction within His Majesty's Dominions. In addition, an applicant was to submit to an examination by "some of the first and most able barristers, advocates and attorneys" in the presence of the Chief Justice or of two or more judges of the Court of Common Pleas and have the certification of the Chief Justice or the judges of his fit capacity and character to be admitted to the practice of law.[12] Comparable provision was made for the qualification of notaries.

These requirements continued in force in Upper Canada when it was carved out of Quebec under the Constitutional Act of 1791, but a more expeditious formula of qualification was prescribed in 1794 to provide a ready body of lawyers. Reminiscent of the provision made by Edward I in 1292 for selection of seven score persons, more or less, to serve the Court of Common Pleas, statutory authority was given to the Governor to license such British subjects, "not exceeding sixteen in number as he shall deem from their probity, education and condition of life best qualified to act as advocates and attornies in the conduct of all legal proceedings in this Province."[13] It appears that licences were granted to the full number; and, in addition, persons admitted under the ordinance of 1785 continued to be entitled to practise.

With the establishment of the Law Society of Upper Canada in 1797, the ordinance of 1785 was repealed, and self-government of the legal profession began. Both aspiring barristers and attorneys were required to register with and

[12] Ordinance of 25 Geo. 3, c. 4.

[13] 1794 (U.C.), c. 4 Further provision for such licensing was made by 1803 (U.C.), c. 3; six licences were authorised and five were issued. The Court of King's Bench purported to admit to practise in 1812 and 1813 but whatever power it had to that end was taken away by 1822 (U.C.), c. 5; see Riddell, "When the Court of King's Bench Broke the Law" (1920) 40 C.L.T. 549.

remain on the books of the Law Society. Five years' articleship or clerkship was prescribed but originally no examination either for initial enrolment as a student at law or for call to the Bar or admission as an attorney; there were, however, the inevitable fees for admission to the Law Society and for the right to practise. The first student was enrolled in 1801. In 1820 provision was made for an entrance examination to provide proof of a liberal education, consisting of " a written translation in the presence of the Society of a portion of one of Cicero's orations or . . . such other exercise as may satisfy the Society of [the applicant's] acquaintance with Latin and English composition."

There had been considerable sentiment at the time of the organisation of the Law Society for a separation of the two branches of the profession and, when the Society was formally incorporated in 1822, attorneys were no longer required to be on its books although the five-year articleship for them remained. Thereafter, they were not subject to any examination and were admissible as before simply upon completing their service and presenting themselves to the court for enrolment. Attempts by the Law Society to prevent the same person from being both barrister and attorney failed because, in one instance, the judges, whose consent to Law Society rules was then required, refused to agree; and, in a second instance, the legislature refused to enact such a measure.[14] However, a system under which Bar standards were gradually being raised (as for example by requiring students to keep four terms and by imposing a Bar examination) while aspiring attorneys needed only a certificate of five years' service could not sensibly continue.

[14] See Riddell, *The Legal Profession in Upper Canada* (1916), pp. 16–19.

The need for change was evident in the number of persons who became attorneys without being called to the Bar; and in 1857 the Law Society's authority was extended to attorneys and solicitors who thenceforward required its certificate of fitness before being admitted by the court.[15]

As in Ontario, so eventually in the other Provinces, certification for call and for admission or for the right to practise as barrister and solicitor became vested in the particular Law Society, but the pertinent question, going to the quality of the legal profession, was what were the standards that had to be met by those who wished to become lawyers. For a lengthy period in the evolution to the modern scheme of legal education judges were involved in the prescribed programmes through statutory requirements of their approval to the governing rules. This was the case, for example, in Ontario until 1872, in Nova Scotia until 1899 and in New Brunswick until 1903.

The statutory authority of the various Law Societies made them responsible for setting standards not only for admission to the practice of law but also for enrolment of persons as students at law and articled clerks. In the latter case, the Law Societies which had at first set their own, rather rudimentary examinations, came to accept school certifications; first, junior matriculation was sufficient, then senior matriculation came to be generally required, then one or two years' successful university work, and now generally an undergraduate college or university degree. Although formally in Ontario two years' college or university work after senior matriculation is the minimum requirement

[15] 1857 (Can.), c. 63.

for admission to a law school, the effective qualification in the Province is a first degree.

So far as legal education or training itself was concerned, the original heavy reliance on apprenticeship—five years was the general standard that prevailed—was not only a matter of following an example, or of emphasising the practical face of the legal profession, but also a recognition of the under-developed condition of higher education in the first half of the 19th century if not beyond that. As soon as institutions of higher learning were established, the Law Societies acknowledged the worth of graduation by reducing the required period of service under articles; for example, in Upper Canada, from five years to three years in 1837; in Nova Scotia from five years to four years until 1872, and thereafter from a general requirement of four years to three for the college graduate; and in New Brunswick the period was first reduced from five years to four years and in 1863 from four years to three years for a college degree holder; but this was modified in 1867 to limit the advantage of a reduced articling period to law graduates only while requiring four years of all others. At all events, there was not such experience in early Canada, or in its later constituents, as occurred in those states of the United States which threw open the legal profession, under a "natural rights" philosophy, to all who might seek entry.[16] Instances did occur in the present century of persons becoming lawyers by special statute but they were exceptional.[17]

Quebec gave particular impetus to the establishment of law schools. Before any of the other Provinces, it provided

[16] See Griswold, *Law and Lawyers in the United States* (1964), pp. 15–20.
[17] See, for example, 1938 (Ont.), c. 57.

in 1836 for a shorter period (four years instead of five) of service under articles for those who had completed studies "in one or several of the seminaries or colleges of the Province or elsewhere." [18] The statute incorporating the Bar of Lower Canada in 1849, besides vesting control of examinations in the new corporation, reduced the clerkship period to three years if the student followed a regular and complete course of study in a college or seminary "and also a regular and complete course of law in any incorporated college or seminary." [19] Three law schools sprang up in the following few years in the wake of this encouragement; an Ecole de Droit in 1851 as a private one-faculty enterprise (which was incorporated in 1852), and a school at McGill University in 1853 and at Laval University in 1854; the latter two have remained in continuous operation since their establishment but the first came to an end in 1867. Laval, indeed, established a branch university and law faculty in Montreal in 1878 which in 1920 became independent and has carried on since as the University of Montreal.

Law Schools in the common law Provinces were a generation in the future. Reading law in a principal's office was no substitute for a systematic legal education; and informal efforts to provide formal instruction by dedicated practitioners who gave occasional lectures simply emphasised the need. The Law Society of Upper Canada opened a law school in 1873 at Osgoode Hall but it collapsed after five years, not so much because attendance was voluntary but because a shorter period of articleship was required of those who did attend and pass the examinations, and this

[18] 1836 (L.C.), c. 10.

[19] See the account by W. S. Johnson, "Legal Education in Quebec" (1905) 4 Can.L.Rev. 451, 491.

indulgence drew students to Toronto to the dismay of benchers and practitioners outside and in the rural areas. The school was re-established in 1881 with no extra credit on articleship, and it faltered a second time because attendance remained optional and the inducement had disappeared. The school was reorganised in 1889 but this time with attendance compulsory. The Law Society had earlier rejected a suggested co-operative arrangement with the University of Toronto, and it operated its own school (not formally named Osgoode Hall Law School until 1924) for the succeeding seventy-nine years until, in 1968, it became a faculty of law, independent of the Law Society, of York University in Toronto.[20]

The Law Society of Upper Canada was not the only organised Bar that ventured to operate a law school. The Law Society of British Columbia offered instruction through a law school in Victoria and another in Vancouver, but as more of a supplement to articling than as a full programme of law study. These schools were not the only route for provincial residents to admission to practise; and after a quarter of a century's experience they were abandoned at

[20] The history of legal education in Ontario is detailed in Bucknall, Baldwin and Lakin, "Pedants, Practitioners and Prophets: Legal Education at Osgoode Hall to 1957" (1968) 6 Osg.H.L.J. 141.

There is an account in it of a short-lived law school established by the Law Society in 1862 (it was closed down in 1868) as an outgrowth of the earlier inauguration of lectures to the students-at-law. Indeed, a shorter-lived law faculty was established by Queen's University in 1861; it collapsed after being refused recognition by the Law Society in 1862; it was revived in 1880 and discontinued again in 1884. The University of Ottawa established a law school in 1887 which also died. Only the University of Toronto managed some continuity in university law studies in Ontario despite occasional interruptions, following the introduction of law as a university discipline in 1843. Professional legal education in Ontario universities finally came alive in 1957.

the outbreak of the Second World War. In 1945, discussions with the University of British Columbia, which had been carried on intermittently over many years, came to a successful conclusion, and a university faculty of law was established with the support and co-operation of the Law Society of British Columbia.

Manitoba tried a different experiment by establishing in 1914 a law school sponsored jointly by its Law Society and by the University of Manitoba, and administered by a board of trustees representing both but with an independent chairman.[21] Here, as in Ontario (where full-time law study was not prescribed until 1949) the concurrent system prevailed, save that for ten years from 1921 full-time attendance was required (with some modification in 1927), to be followed by a year under articles. The concurrent system was resumed in 1931 and continued until a decision was taken in 1964, influenced by the developments in Ontario, to establish a full-time three-year programme under the control of a faculty of law in the University of Manitoba, and to be followed by one year of service under articles and some clinical training in a Bar admission course.

In both Alberta and Saskatchewan formal legal education rested from the beginning with its universities. A faculty of law was established in the University of Alberta in 1912, and instruction was given in Calgary until 1921 when the present school was opened on the campus of the University at Edmonton. The College of Law in the University of Saskatchewan was established in 1913.

In New Brunswick, formal legal education began in a

[21] See the account in Williams, " Legal Education in Manitoba, 1913–1950 " (1950) 28 Can. Bar Rev. 759, 880.

law school established there in 1892 by the University of King's College of Windsor, Nova Scotia, and the school obtained full recognition for its graduates from the Barristers' Society of New Brunswick, through legislation in 1901. The University of New Brunswick absorbed this school into a faculty of law in 1923. It continued with the existing system of concurrent office training until 1950 when it met the then Canadian norm of full-time law study.[22]

Dalhousie Law School, established in 1883, can properly be regarded as the oldest law school, and the first university law school, with a professional as well as a liberal orientation, in the common law Provinces. For more than half a century, it provided intellectual leadership in the critical study of the common law in Canada, but its remoteness from the centres of population of Canada, the continuing strength of the apprenticeship tradition and the handicap of a small full-time teaching staff softened its impact elsewhere in Canada. When its Dean, Dr. D. A. MacRae, moved to Osgoode Hall Law School as a full-time lecturer in 1924 and that school began to strengthen its teaching faculty under newly appointed Dean John D. Falconbridge, while at the same time a concurrent system of law school and law office attendance was maintained in the only law school until 1949 permitted to qualify students in Ontario for law practice, a policy was set for a quarter of a century that ultimately engendered the fiercest debate on legal education that Canada has hitherto known.

The policy was intended to demonstrate that the proper mix for a lawyer's education was to balance apprentice-

[22] See the account in McAllister, " Some Phases of Legal Education in New Brunswick " (1955) 8 U.N.B.L.J. 33.

ship with concurrent academic work, but not to give any ascendant position to the academic programme. So long as the law was measured by a purely professional practitioner approach the system had the merit of at least providing some critical analysis. However, it could not work under any wider view of the law and its function. Even as it was, not only were students caught in a squeeze between law school and office work, but academic standards, if they extended beyond the purely positivist approach, either had to be compromised by good teachers or left to be administered by poor ones. In this respect, English universities, teaching law without being tied to Inns of Court or Law Society requirements, were much better off from the standpoint of scholarship and scholarly writing. It was on this very basis that the University of Toronto offered a liberal arts and law programme for some two decades notwithstanding the refusal of the Law Society to credit any of the work for the right to practise.

A clash of principle within and without Osgoode Hall Law School, which had been building up for more than a decade, broke into the open early in 1949. A limited but steady movement towards emphasis of the academic programme and de-emphasis of the uncertain and uneven results of concurrent apprenticeship had been encouraged since the end of the Second World War; but an announced revival of law office training in the education of a lawyer led to the resignation of most of the full-time teaching staff. Dean Wright, whose name and memory will ever be associated with the liberalisation of legal education in Canada—for which he fought in the interests of the legal profession itself no less than in the interests of the consumers of legal services—joined the Faculty of Law at the University of Toronto with two of his colleagues. For the next eight years, that Faculty, given partial recognition by the Law Society in 1949, sought equality of status with Osgoode Hall Law School. Resolution of the issue, which had national proportions and certainly international attention, came in 1957 when the Law Society of Upper Canada agreed to full recognition of university law faculties that could meet certain conditions as to student eligibility and programme for the full-time study of law.[23]

The Law Society never did implement the policy the announcement of which in 1949 led to the resignation of Dean Wright and others. Instead, it took the previously opposed path to full-time academic study; and with the growing numbers that were seeking places in a law school, its monopoly position became physically untenable as it had become intellectually indefensible. Three university law schools, in addition to that at the University of Toronto, were established in 1957 in Ontario: at Queen's University, the University of Western Ontario and the University of Ottawa, respectively; a fourth, which became the sixth in Ontario, was established at the University of Windsor in 1967. The final act in the drama of upheaval was performed in 1968 when, as previously mentioned, Osgoode Hall Law School was, with the approval of the Law Society, taken over by York University as its faculty of law.

What has emerged in Canada in legal education is uniformity in the structure attending the process of qualification for law practice: conditions of admissibility to a law school are fairly uniform; full-time students are taught by

[23] For fuller detail on the conflict, see Wright, " Should the Profession Control Legal Education? " (1950) 3 Jo.Leg.Ed. 1; and also the study cited in note 20.

full-time staff albeit there are some part-time instructors; graduation from the three-year law school is followed by an articling period which is, in the main, one year, but is nine months in Nova Scotia and six in New Brunswick.[24] In some Provinces, there are organised Bar admission programmes of varying duration and quality, conducted either after or concurrently with the clerkship period, in emulation of the pioneer programme in Ontario which is the best organised and most demanding (it involves a series of examinations on the work) and runs for about six months after the articling period. In Prince Edward Island and in Newfoundland where there are no law schools, a law school degree is recognised as a qualification for practice with the required supplement of articling periods of eighteen months and nine months, respectively, not all of which need be after law school graduation.

Canada's bi-legal and bilingual endowment has given rise to a civil law school in a common law Province, Ontario, and a common law programme in Quebec, each recognised for admission to the Quebec and Ontario bars, respectively. The University of Ottawa, which has a common law school, had earlier established a civil law school which is operated separately as to faculty and programme; and its graduates are accredited for practice in Quebec on the same basis as those of this Province's now four law schools. McGill, which had long ago tried an LL.B. programme but had dropped it in 1924 because apprenticeship requirements at

[24] For an analytical and statistical account of Canadian legal education, see Cohen, "The Condition of Legal Education in Canada" (1950) 28 Can. Bar Rev. 266; also Cohen, "The Condition of Legal Education in Canada—Fifteen Years Later 1949–1964" (1964) *Canadian Bar Association Papers* 116.

the time made it difficult for common law students to study law outside their own Provinces, recently reinstated a common law course, and obtained recognition from the Law Society of Upper Canada in 1968 (with the concurrence of the law schools in Ontario) for its LL.B. graduates in 1969 and beyond. There is no separate administration as at the University of Ottawa, nor is there a strictly separate faculty for the common law studies.

Legal Scholarship and Research in Canada

England is proof of the fact that scholarly work in and about the law and the legal system is not dependent on the professionalisation of law studies, whatever be the intellectual standards of such studies. But the American example, reinforcing the English, and providing leads for the English universities as well as for those of Canada, demonstrates how much more, and more effectively, the blend of a university's open approach with a tough professionally orientated curriculum can accomplish in making the law more socially responsive and directive and in effecting improvements in its administration. Apart from the retention in Canada of the articling element for Bar qualification, the Canadian law schools are much closer in organisation and curriculum to those in the United States than to those in England; and the influence of the excellent American graduate programmes, at Harvard, Yale, Columbia, Berkeley, Michigan and elsewhere, to which the vast majority of present-day Canadian law teachers have been exposed, has had a pronounced impact on Canadian law teaching methods and on the range of materials thought appropriate for study in a law school.

The past ten years has seen an increase in the number of legal perodicals published in Canada; in the gross but not relative (to number of full-time law teachers) volume of scholarly writing; and in the number of graduate and research programmes offered in Canadian law schools. It would have been odd were it otherwise. Case books have proliferated, some monographs have been written, research projects on a variety of problems are engaging many law teachers, but Canadian texts on such basic subjects as torts, contracts, criminal law, and administrative law, to mention but a few that are needed are still to be written for the common law lawyer. The civilians in Quebec are a little better off in this respect.

English judicial dominance brought in its train, not only the English law reports, but also English texts, English digests and other practitioner tools; and they gained an ascendancy and a following at a time when Canadian scholarship was barely awakening. Canadian periodicals in the 19th century, like the *Canada Law Journal* and the *Canadian Law Times* (both of which surrendered at the end of 1922 to the then incipient *Canadian Bar Review*), were catholic in their coverage, regularly reporting on decisions and other legal developments in the United States as well as reporting cases and noting other matters of legal interest in Canada and in the United Kingdom. Although they provided a forum for Canadian writing, there was in them a substantial element of the anecdotal, which may have contributed to the camaraderie of the Bar but could also be beguiling. In the circumstances of the time, it was probably too much to expect either original Canadian contributions to legal scholarship or much comprehensive or critical writing on legal subjects from a purely Canadian standpoint.

Canada did not have the impetus to native works that American independence provided for its neighbour to the south. The record is not, however, completely barren.

Very little Canadian legal writing appeared before the middle of the 19th century. An early work of monumental proportions for the period was Beamish Murdoch's *Epitome of the Laws of Nova Scotia*, published in four volumes, two in each of the years 1832 and 1833.[25] A portion of the preface puts it in perspective; the author wrote:

> "The variety of instances in which our provincial acts and usages have altered the laws of England, and the uncertainty as to what English acts are or are not in force here, suggested to the writer the usefulness of a work in humble imitation of the Commentaries of Blackstone, retaining such English law as we have adopted, and adding under each head or chapter the substance of provincial enactments that belonged to it. . . . The author has been favored with a reading of the Commentaries by Mr. Kent on American law, and has found them of much service in preparing this work."

Whether this *Epitome* had any extra-provincial influence is uncertain. It is not, and does not appear to have been among the holdings of the library of the Law Society of Upper Canada, and it is not even mentioned in the comprehensive (but by no means complete) bibliography of Canadian law by Reynald Boult, published in 1966. The American vogue for Blackstone, evidenced by local editions, abridgments and summaries, does not appear to have been followed in Canada. A Canadian adaptation, edited by Alexander Leith, appeared in 1864 and a second edition

[25] See Harvey, "Nova Scotia's Blackstone" (1933) 11 Can. Bar Rev. 339.

co-edited with James F. Smith was published in 1880. Thereafter, E. D. Armour took over the work which, because of statutory and other changes became, with consent, *Armour on Real Property*, first published in 1901, and reaching a second edition in 1916. It is still consulted, which is itself a commentary on the Ontario law of real property. In 1896, R. E. Kingsford published an adaptation of part of Blackstone to the law of Ontario. Nothing further appears to have been done with Blackstone's *Commentaries* in Canada. It has become a book on which to reminisce.

In the last quarter of the 19th century and in the early part of the succeeding one, there were numerous examples of a Canadian penchant for mounting Canadian material on non-Canadian texts. Taylor's *Commentaries on Equity Jurisprudence*, published in 1876, was founded on Story. Leith adapted to Ontario law in 1881 Joshua Williams' *Principles of the Law of Real Property*. Beal's *Law of Bailments* was published in 1900 with notes of Canadian Cases by A. C. Forster Boulton, who also produced Canadian editions of *Fisher on Mortgages* in 1910, *Oswald on Contempt of Court* in 1911, and *Ross on Discovery* in 1912. The seventh edition of *Theobald on Wills* was supplemented by *Notes of Canadian Statutes and Cases* by E. D. Armour in 1908. Mr. Justice Russell of the Nova Scotia Supreme Court, renowned also as a law teacher at Dalhousie, provided Canadian notes in 1910 to the third edition of *Blackburn on Sales*; and he did the same in respect of the fifth edition of *Fry on Specific Performance* in 1911. The fourth edition of *Clerk and Lindsell on Torts* was issued in 1908 with Canadian notes; and, more ambitiously, a companion volume, entitled *Canadian Law of Contracts*, was published in connection with the sixteenth edition of *Chitty on Contracts* in 1914. A Canadian condensed version of *Jarman on Wills*, by R. E. Kingsford, who had other writing credits to his name, was published in 1913.

All this was useful parasitism for practitioners; it was not much of a contribution to scholarship in the various subjects. Of the original Canadian works that were published in the latter part of the 19th century and in the early part of the 20th, many were concerned with various aspects of property; books on dower (which still obtains in Ontario and in the maritime Provinces), on landlord and tenant, on mortgages of land and on vendor and purchaser were among them. Digests and statute citators, answering recurring needs, also abounded in this period and still abound for their utility.

A few volumes in this span of time could be counted scholarly. J. S. Ewart's *Estoppel by Misrepresentation*, published in 1900, simultaneously in Canada, England and the United States, was one of them; as was also his book on *Waiver Distributed*, published by the Harvard University Press in 1917 with a foreword by Dean Roscoe Pound. Alpheus Todd, born in England, who emigrated to Canada as a youth and became Parliamentary Librarian at Ottawa, produced among other writings, two leading works of international repute, *Parliamentary Government in England*, published in 1867, and *Parliamentary Government in the British Colonies*, published in 1880. The early years of the 20th century saw the initial venture into law book writing by John D. Falconbridge, later to become an internationally respected scholar in the conflict of laws. His *Law of Mortgages* which he saw through three editions (the last in 1942) was first published in 1919; and his *Banking and Bills of Exchange* which he saw through six editions (the last in 1956; a seventh was published recently, and after his death, under the editorship of A. W. Rogers), was first published in 1907. His collected *Essays on the Conflict of Laws* appeared in 1947.

Although Halsbury's *Laws of England*, of which the first volume of the first edition appeared in 1907, and the *English and Empire Digest*, which began publication in 1919, undoubtedly strengthened the continuing attachment of the Canadian courts and legal profession to English law, it cannot be said that they exercised any special discouraging influence on the preparation of Canadian legal monographs. In such particular statutory areas as mining law, shipping law and railway law, Canadian texts appeared to fill gaps. None were needed as badly in the old common law fields where English texts were in adequate supply. Unless the Canadian text was first class, and able to compete in a wider market, there did not seem to be much point in providing more of the same under a Canadian imprint; certainly not unless there was a case to be made for a Canadian approach to the particular subject, sufficiently marked off from the English to be distinguishable; and this depended largely on the courts and partly on the legislature.

What has happened in the past half-century, and certainly in the past quarter-century, is a concentration on periodical writing to express the growing Canadianisation of our law. The law review article and the case comment have become the staples of the legal scholarship of the law teachers in Canada, and the various law reviews have become, quite markedly, their organs of opinion. Their contributions are leavened, however, by pieces from members of the Bar, especially in the *Canadian Bar Review*. With more than 300 full-time law teachers now in the various Canadian law faculties, the members of the Bar may not feel as deep an obligation to as full a measure of periodical writing as they did when the *Canada Law Journal* (which began before Confederation) and the *Canadian Law Times* (which first appeared in 1881) were in competition. But their role in legal writing is an important one, if only to reflect the professional approach, which cannot be ignored in any philosophising about law and the legal system.

The case comment as developed in Canadian periodical literature lacks the brevity of the Notes in the *Law Quarterly Review*, and the terseness and compactness of the Recent Cases section of American periodicals like the *Harvard Law Review*. It is longer and more developed than the former, and looser or more discursive than the latter but not nearly as ambitious as the Notes or Comment sections of American periodicals. Refined during the late Dr. Wright's editorship of the *Canadian Bar Review*, and continued during the editorships of Professor Nicholls and now of Professor Castel, it was a sharp tool for analysing judicial expositions of principle for internal consistency, comparative merit and value standards. The purpose was constructive, even if this did not always emerge very clearly to the judge or court whose opinion was being dissected; and the focus on a particular case or line of cases could have an immediate professional impact which a general textbook could not always match. However, the overriding question, important here as in respect of periodical literature generally, was whether it would be considered by the courts or read by the judges. It could always be adopted by the barrister as his own if he was unable or unwilling to cite it.

The issue is an old one and perhaps no longer worth

even cursory notice.[26] The remarks of a former Chief Justice of Canada in a Reference proceeding in 1950 that " the *Canadian Bar Review* is not an authority in this Court " and hence not to be quoted, is reminiscent of some words attributed to Lord Haldane, when Sir Robert Finlay cited Halsbury's *Laws of England* in a Canadian Privy Council appeal; the attributed words were these: " so far as I am concerned I have already expressed the opinion and I express it once again—this work is edited by a very eminent lawyer, and several eminent lawyers have written it, but I protest against it being cited as an authority, and I may say that it is not to be cited here again." [27] I venture to say that such remarks about any book of repute or established legal periodical would be considered quaint today in any Canadian court; the concern would be only with relevance and the court would, of course, assess weight.

The character of legal writing in Canada as elsewhere is undergoing change as the affirmative or positive role of the law is evolving—to a larger degree than before through legislative action—and as the relationship between law and other social sciences is being more thoroughly investigated and their reciprocal influence encouraged. Legal analysis should not suffer in this; rather it should become sharper. Law school libraries are beginning to mirror the growing social science sophistication of the law teacher. Canadian law libraries, in general, have, however, a long way to go before they can claim to be fully adequate for even Canadian historical research, let alone comparative research in the

26 See Nicholls, " Legal Periodicals and the Supreme Court of Canada " (1950) 28 Can. Bar Rev. 422.

27 See (1920) 56 C.L.J. 294. I have been unable to identify the case in which this was allegedly said.

common law or comparative research in the civil and common law systems. No law school library in Canada has as yet more than 100,000 volumes; most have half or a little better than half that number. The two largest law libraries in Canada are the Supreme Court of Canada library which has about 130,000 volumes in both the civil law and the common law and the library of the Law Society of Upper Canada which is a little smaller with well over 100,000 volumes. Inter-library loan services can help the research efforts of particular students, but the range of graduate and research studies that can be offered in Canada must necessarily be limited until there are adequate library resources to support wider or more varied programmes.

Research has, over the past few years, been melded with law reform as governments have begun to appreciate the need for systematic and continuous oversight of the functioning of the law. Ontario pioneered this by the establishment in 1964 of the Ontario Law Reform Commission, with authority to initiate projects as well as to undertake matters referred to it by the Attorney-General. Projects completed include a report on limitation of actions, on the protection of privacy, and on the trade sale of new houses. Projects on foot, which are of major proportions, include family law, the law of property, and the law of evidence. The Institute of Law Research and Reform was established in late 1967 in Alberta as a co-operative venture of the Government, the Law Society of Alberta and the University of Alberta, with its base in the University. It has already completed its first project, a report on Compensation for Victims of Crime. In 1968 the Legal Research Institute of the University of Manitoba was established, with representation thereon of the Government of the Province, the Law Society of

Manitoba and the Faculty of Law. It too has completed its first research report, one on Privacy and the Law. There has been federal government interest in a continuing law reform agency at the federal level but it is still under consideration.

The foregoing developments have added another dimension to the law teacher, because it is on him that chief reliance has so far been placed to conduct or direct the research of these law reform agencies. None has a legal staff like that of the English Law Commission, although the Ontario Law Reform Commission has a counsel, and the Director of the Alberta agency has a legally trained assistant. In Quebec, where the first full-scale revision of the Civil Code is under way, after a century's operation, the head of the Office of Revision is also a law teacher, Professor Paul Crepeau of the Faculty of Law of McGill University.

Although law reform is at the present time in the hands of lawyers alone, it is not likely to remain so; and other disciplines will be joined in group efforts as the problems calling for legal treatment become more complex. The law schools, having broken from one type of narrowness in their approach to law, may be expected to be sensitive to the danger of a different kind of narrowness that lies in believing that lawyers alone should make the judgments that are reflected in complex regulatory schemes. There is already evidence, in their appointments and in their research work, that they understand the interdisciplinary character of many contemporary problems that might be labelled legal simply because they are to be solved by legislation. Urban or community planning, regional conservation, water control, and pollution are illustrations of matters that need the architect, the economist, the sociologist, the engineer as well as the lawyer; and if the latter sits at the centre because the end result will be legislative or packaged in a private or inter-governmental agreement, his legal skills will not alone be enough to provide the necessary background to the legal framework which must grow out of the non-legal data.

The Influence of The United States

American influence on Canadian law has been more perceptible in the legislative field than in the judicial. Mechanics' lien legislation, homestead laws, labour relations legislation, oil and gas laws, legislation for the regulation of security trading, corporation legislation, fair accommodation practices and fair employment practices statutes, and personal property security legislation are well known areas of Canadian obligation to American example.[28] Inevitably, Canadian courts now freed of compelled subservience to English decision will look more to decisions in the United States. It is not only that social and economic ties will prove to be as persuasive as were the historical and constitutional ties with Great Britain; but Canadian law school teachers, now bringing American law into their classrooms as a result of personal experience as well as for pedagogical reasons, are making American decisions and their sources familiar to future members of the Canadian legal profession and of the bench.

[28] Mowat in his lecture referred to in note 33, *infra*, had this to say at p. 6:

> "Our Legislature has also adopted and sometimes with little alteration many valuable American statutes. . . . Instances of such statutes are those abolishing the old law of primogeniture, regulating chattel mortgages, limited partnerships and the sale of infants' estates by the Court of Chancery—and others."

There is the overriding fact that American law deserves notice for its merit; and certainly as it is reflected in the many scholarly texts and monographs; in such fully researched volumes as the various *Restatements*; and in much of the periodical literature (of which there is a completely unmanageable quantity). The superb law library resources that exist in so many places, and especially in many of the leading law schools in the United States represent common law holdings in English materials, and in those of other members of the Commonwealth, that are beyond compare either in Canada and perhaps in England as well. England itself could be counted indebted to the United States in the 19th century for such books as *Greenleaf on Evidence*, on which Taylor was based, and *Rawle on Covenants for Title*, and certainly for *Story on Equity Jurisprudence*. In Canada, *Wigmore on Evidence* has, for a considerable time, been a standard reference in the courts in that branch of the law; and *Scott on Trusts* is also frequently used. *Prosser on Torts* was often cited until in the past decade it has given way to Fleming whose book on torts, based on broad common law sources including Canadian as well as American decisions, is by far the one most used in argument to the Court of Appeal of Ontario and by that court itself when it has occasion to refer to a textbook on the subject. It appears to be frequently used in other Canadian provincial courts as well.

However limited or discriminating has been or is the use of American writings in Canadian courts—and I have referred only to a few works that can be considered classics—the references to such sources in Canadian law schools, certainly in the common law ones, are extensive and constant.

Superb teaching materials have come from American legal scholars, and Canadian teachers quite rightly see enormous advantage in using them, or at least referring to them in association with their own materials. Any examination of American writings whether in texts or monographs or in casebooks, on such basic subjects as contracts, torts and property, both real and personal, will bear out their usefulness for the study of problems in those fields arising under Canadian law. The list could be extended to include evidence, corporation law, conflict of laws and commercial law, if not the run of the curriculum.

English courts gave cautious encouragement to references to American reports in the first half of the 19th century. Patteson J., in the Court of Queen's Bench in *Beverley* v. *Lincoln Gas Light and Coke Co.* decided in 1837, said that decisions of courts in the United States were " intrinsically entitled to the highest respect," but could not be cited as direct authority in English proceedings.[29] There were other such encomiums; but in 1877 James L.J. in the English Court of Appeal in *The North British and Mercantile Insurance Co.* v. *The London Liverpool and Globe Insurance Co.* replied to counsel's attempt to cite American state court decisions, on a point on which there were allegedly no English cases, by demolishing American state courts and Canadian provincial courts in one composite blow. He is reported as saying this [30]:

> " We shall be glad to hear any case of the Supreme Court in America, but can the decisions of the State Court stand higher than a decision of the Court in

[29] (1837) 6 Ad. & E. 829 at p. 837, 112 E.R. 318 at p. 321.
[30] (1877) 44 L.J.Ch. 537 at p. 538.

> Nova Scotia, for example, which could not be cited here? "

A dozen years later, Lord Halsbury in *Re Missouri Steamship Co.* prevented counsel from quoting a judgment of the Supreme Court of the United States, apparently feeling that it was being put forward as an authority, " in the same way as if they were decisions of our Courts," and this, he said, was wrong.[31] His associates on the Court, Fry and Cotton L.JJ., struck broadside at citation of American cases as being a waste of time and as meriting protest. Nonetheless, the court did discuss American law in the judgments that were delivered.

This English insularity is a thing of the past, and the highest court as well as courts of first instance cite not only American decisions, but on occasion, Canadian cases as well.[32] However, it appears to have had an inhibiting effect on the citation of American decisions by Canadian courts, which had been growing, and was particularly (and for understandable historical reasons) evident in the courts of the Maritime Provinces in respect of decisions from the New England states.

In a published extract of a lecture in 1857 on the use of American decisions in Canadian courts Oliver Mowat (who had not only a distinguished but an unusual career, retiring from the Bench to become Premier of Ontario for a continuous period of almost twenty-five years) fully supported the resort to American cases (never, however, on matters of practice he said), but only where the English and

31 (1889) 42 Ch.D. 321 at p. 330.

32 Recent instances are *Warner* v. *Metropolitan Police Commissioner* [1968] 2 All E.R. 356 and *Re Figgis* [1968] 1 All E.R. 999.

Canadian authorities on a relevant point left it in doubt.[33] He felt that this was sanctioned, as he put it, "by the authority and example of the best English Judges and Jurists," although he did go on to say that "in Canada we must find advantage and interest in examining [American] decisions and writings far beyond what is the case in England [because] our local circumstances are more nearly like those of the people of the United States." It is this last sentiment that is the relevant one today.

There seemed to be good reason, on this ground, after Confederation, to examine decisions under the federal constitution of the United States for their value for Canadian federalism, making any proper allowances for differences in underlying theory or formulation. This, indeed, was the attitude of some of the judges of the Supreme Court of Canada in its early years. In *Bank of Toronto* v. *Lambe* in 1887, the Privy Council discouraged reference to constitutional decisions of the Supreme Court of the United States.[34] I would think, however, that those decisions would be more apt to be helpful on the scope of the federal trade and commerce power in Canada, for example, than the Act of Union of England and Scotland upon which the Privy Council relied in this connection in 1881.[35] Despite the Privy Council, there have been occasional references in Canadian constitutional cases to American Supreme Court decisions—even by the Privy Council itself[36]—but it may

33 Observations on the Use and Value of American Reports in reference to Canadian Jurisprudence (1857) 3 U.C.L.J.(o.s.) 3.

34 (1887) 12 App.Cas. 575 at p. 587.

35 *Citizens Insurance Co.* v. *Parsons* (1881) 7 App.Cas. 96 at p. 112.

36 See, for example, *Att.-Gen. Ontario* v. *Reciprocal Insurers* [1924] A.C. 328 at p. 338, referring to a United States Supreme Court decision that was later overruled.

be that interpretation has hardened to the point where frequent references would be unthinkable, short of a fundamental shift in the judicial philosophy of the Canadian Constitution.

The history of citation of American cases by Canadian courts is a long one, as a study published in 1966 reveals.[37] In addition to the reasons already noted for advertence to American cases, the study makes the significant point that since neither the United States nor the constituent units of a later Canada had moved very far away from English law in the first half of the 19th century, there was nothing particularly liberal or revolutionary in looking at expositions of law that was close to English law, and hence to Canadian law. The latter stayed closer to English law than did the American legislatures and courts, and citation of American cases abated in frequency by the second quarter of the 20th century.

The areas of citation in recent years suggest that the practical reason for referring to American cases, namely, the want of other authority on the subject, dominates the election to do so. This was the case in the 19th century in such fields as mining and insurance. There has been similar experience in the present century in insurance, and now also in oil and gas problems (in Alberta particularly), in the field of restitution, in the conflict of laws, in connection with international legal issues, and even on the law of negligence. New facts situations, although involving old principles, for example, the use or non-use of seat belts in an automobile, can, of course, be expected to provoke a

[37] See MacIntyre, "The Use of American Cases in Canadian Courts" (1966) 2 U.B.C.L.Rev. 478.

search for analogues in other common law jurisdictions, not only the United States, but it is there that they can usually be found; the variety of American life and the multiplicity of jurisdictions ensures this. Warning against indiscriminate use of American decisions is not necessary for Canadian courts; they have been quite selective in their references.

A check of the volumes of the *Dominion Law Reports* published for the years 1948, 1958 and 1968 shows this quite clearly. In the four volumes for 1948 there were 403 Canadian cases reported and American cases were cited in fifteen of them; but in the same volumes, seven cases cited Australian decisions and eight cited New Zealand decisions. In the four volumes published in 1958, 385 Canadian cases were reported, and in seventeen there were citations of American decisions; there were three cases referring to Australian decisions, and single case references to a number of other foreign jurisdictions. In 1968, six volumes of reports were published containing a total of 575 Canadian cases; American decisions were cited in twenty-one cases, Australian decisions were cited in twelve, and New Zealand decisions were cited in ten. The citations in the three test years were either of approval, or disapproval, or the cited cases were distinguished or merely referred to. The classes of cases in which the most frequent American citations were found were negligence and insurance cases; and other branches of law fairly well represented were conflict of laws, carrier liability, contracts, trusts and evidence. Australian and New Zealand citations were most frequent in taxation, criminal law and descent and distribution.

No conclusions can be drawn from so limited an appraisal other than the obvious one that Canadian courts are hospitable to cases from other common law jurisdictions, and that, English cases apart, American decisions are the most frequently cited from such other jurisdictions. The inclination of counsel in this matter is, of course, important; and their training and experience may be what is reflected in the picture I have presented. The frequency of citation is bound to increase, probably beyond the obvious resort on points on which both English and Canadian decisions are lacking. *Stare decisis* apart, it is the fitness of the solutions to legal issues offered by the cases and not their source that should be the moving consideration of their value.

4

THE BRITISH TRADITION AND CANADIAN FEDERALISM

THE creation of the Canadian federation under the British North America Act 1867 did not involve an abrupt break with the past. Not only was there a common understanding that the existing forms and style of responsible government would be followed—it seemed sufficient to say in the preamble to the Act that the federal union would have a constitution "similar in principle to that of the United Kingdom"—but section 129 preserved all laws in force in the confederating units, and continued the existence and powers of all courts and officers, except as otherwise provided by the Act and subject also to alteration of existing arrangements by the federal Parliament or by a provincial legislature in accordance with the distribution of power prescribed by the Act of Union.

In a geographic or territorial sense, the colonial Provinces retained their separate identities; and the functional limitations imposed by the federal Constitution were to be applied in the future to the common law and civil law developments that had taken place in the common law Provinces and in Quebec respectively. For Quebec, particularly, the scheme of allocation of law-making power raised the question how far civil law concepts would be recognised in the enactment of federal legislation [1]; and, again, how far judicial exposition

[1] See, for example, Mignault, "The Dominion Succession Duty Act: Its Effect on the Succession Law of Quebec" (1941) 19 Can. Bar Rev. 733.

of the law would, apart from legislation, be influenced by that scheme in respect of matters that fell within federal competence. The historical division that had prevailed in pre-1867 Canada—in the united Province created in 1840—between the law applicable in Lower Canada and that applicable in Upper Canada was altered by the new constitution of 1867 so far as a national cast was given to some matters which had been dealt with either under the civil law or under the common law according to area of operation; for example, marriage and divorce, commercial paper, rights and liabilities of carriers. In this connection, the role of the Supreme Court of Canada became important when that Court was established by federal statute in 1875.

The function of the Supreme Court and of the Privy Council (during the period that it was the final appellate authority) as unifying courts for the common law Provinces, served to recall the prospect, raised by section 94 of the British North America Act, for federal legislation for the uniformity of the laws relative to property and civil rights in those Provinces and of the procedure of the courts thereof. This unique federal power was, however, dependent for its effect on the previous adoption by any common law Province of the federal statute. A study of this constitutional provision for exclusive federal competence in exercises of uniformity has shown that it is a dead letter, not likely to be revived.[2] Uniformity on the common law level is thus a matter of ultimate judicial decision. On the legislative level, there is the Canada-wide embrace of federal legislation (although, of course, the federal Parliament may limit the territorial

[2] See Scott, "Section 94 of the B.N.A. Act" (1942) 20 Can. Bar Rev. 525.

application of its enactments), and, as among the Provinces, there is the voluntary co-operation for uniform legislation, symbolised since 1918 in the Conference of Commissioners on Uniformity of Legislation in Canada, consisting of representatives of the various Provinces and of Canada itself, whose object is to promote uniformity of legislation (where practicable) and which has drafted a variety of model statutes to that end for adoption.[3]

Federalism for Canada added a dimension to the authority of the courts, although there was nothing in the written Constitution to say so. Unlike the situation in England or in Great Britain as a whole where, *Bonham's* case and the Numerals case[4] notwithstanding, the courts may interpret but not invalidate parliamentary legislation, courts in the Canadian hierarchy understood from the beginning that it fell to them (whether as implicit in the Constitution or as a unique principle—perhaps even a common law one—of judicial power in a federation) to determine the limits of the exercises of power by limited legislatures.[5]

The limitations required a reassessment not only of the source of legislative authority in private law but also in public law, using this phrase to gather in those matters that immediately after the British conquest would have been regarded as subject to English law and not to the French civil law. The respective lists of legislative powers gave

[3] See MacTavish, "Uniformity of Legislation in Canada—An Outline" (1947) 25 Can. Bar Rev. 36. Quebec is the only Province that has not adopted any uniform statute, in whole or in part.

[4] *Bonham's Case* (1610) 8 Co.Rep. 113b at p. 118a; 77 E.R. 646 at p. 652; *MacCormick* v. *Lord Advocate*, 1953 S.C. 396.

[5] See Strayer, *Judicial Review of Legislation in Canada* (1968), Chaps. 1 and 2.

little, if any, lead on this issue; clarity to a degree was achieved in vesting in the national Parliament exclusive legislative authority in relation to the criminal law and criminal procedure, which included evidence in criminal matters. It will be recalled that the English criminal law, introduced with English law generally in 1764, survived the Quebec Act of 1774, and may be said to have achieved a national character, so to speak, even before Confederation. The criminal law and the procedure connected therewith would not, however, represent all relations between the Crown and its subjects.[6]

The position of the Crown itself was nowhere stated in the British North America Act, either from the standpoint of the impact thereon of legislative power or of judicial power.

Presumably, the common law rules applied but there remained the question of the extent to which they could be fitted into a constitutional scheme that envisaged the Crown at two executive and legislative levels, and functioning in different areas at each of those levels.

Over and above all else in the Canadian Constitution, there was the stark fact that it was a British statute and that it would be interpreted ultimately by a British-based and British-oriented court, which would likely bring to bear upon it all the standards and techniques of the British judicial tradition. In this, Canada has not been disappointed; it

[6] The importance of the distinction between public law and private law for Quebec was noticed by Walton, " The Legal System of Quebec " (1913) 33 C.L.J. 280. For example, the law of Crown liability and that governing the liability of public officials for wrongful exercise of authority is of English origin.

would have been perhaps miraculous had something different come from the Privy Council.[7]

The Judicial Power in Canada

Unlike the later constitution of Australia, the Canadian Constitution nowhere mentioned appeals to the Privy Council, nor did it give constitutional status to the existence and jurisdiction of the Supreme Court of Canada as did the Australian Constitution to the High Court of that country and as did the United States Constitution to the Supreme Court of that federal state. The Supreme Court of Canada is a purely statutory court with a jurisdiction dependent on federal legislation; and, in that dependence, on the meaning of the words of section 101 of the British North America Act authorising Parliament to " provide for the constitution, maintenance and organization of a general court of appeal for Canada." Until their abolition, Privy Council appeals, by leave and as of right, were founded on both the Privy Council Acts of 1833 and 1844 and on local legislation which had been authorised to that end. It proved beneficial after all not to have had Privy Council appellate authority spelled out in the British North America Act. Through the combined effect of the Statute of Westminster 1931 and section 101 already mentioned, a simple federal statute was enough to displace the Privy Council in favour of the Supreme Court of Canada.[8]

The Supreme Court of Canada is more than a federal

[7] The point is made by Jennings, " Constitutional Interpretation—The Experience of Canada " (1937) 51 Harv.L.Rev. 1 at p. 35.

[8] Federal authority to enact such a statute was certified by the Privy Council itself in *Att.-Gen. Ontario* v. *Att.-Gen. Canada* [1947] A.C. 127.

court in the style of the Supreme Court of the United States; it is a national court, able to hear appeals on matters of provincial law as well as of federal law, as is the High Court of Australia. Further, because its jurisdiction is statutory only, the legislation governing it can limit appeals or impose conditions upon which they may be brought; and the power given to Parliament in respect of the Supreme Court is wide enough to entitle it to authorise appeals from provincial courts on matters within provincial legislative competence even if the Province purports to make the provincial court judgment final.[9]

There are two features of the judicial provisions of the Canadian Constitution which have uniqueness. First, there is the provision that the judges of the superior, county and district courts of the Provinces are to be federally appointed and paid, although the courts themselves are to be constituted and organised by the respective Provinces.[10] The records indicate that this was, to some extent at least, a reflection of the anticipated affluence of the new Dominion as contrasted with the limited resources that the Provinces would command.

What has resulted from this reposing of judicial appointments to certain provincial courts in the federal government is a limited type of " separation of powers " problem affecting the provincial administration. If, to take an example, a provincial superior court is to be identified by what it does and not by what it is called, then functions associated with it would have to be discharged by a federal appointee; and hence to vest them in a provincial administrative tribunal

[9] See *Crown Grain Co.* v. *Day* [1908] A.C. 504.
[10] British North America Act 1867, ss. 92 (14), 96 and 100.

operated by provincial appointees would be to the extent of such vesting unconstitutional. A good deal of conceptualism crept into this issue.[11] However, the recent course of decision, especially in the Supreme Court of Canada, indicates that a pragmatic approach has taken over, and that provincial administrative agencies will be judged not only by what they do (even if it is analogous to jurisdiction exercised by a superior court at confederation or later) but as well by how they do it (that is, by a procedure unlike that of a court in the strict sense) and by the purpose to be served (for example, the administration of a social insurance scheme as in workmen's compensation, rather than the determination of individual liability).[12] History has also been invoked to permit the Provinces to create and staff small debt courts which, as they existed before confederation, were not in the categories of superior, county or district courts.

The second uniquity is the conferring of power upon the Parliament of Canada to establish courts "for the better administration of the laws of Canada." The phrase "laws of Canada" has been interpreted to mean federal law only, and not to include laws in force in Canada through provincial enactment.[13] There is no reason in principle why it should not also include such common law or civil law principles as were in force at confederation and which after-

[11] The classical examination of this issue is Willis, "Section 96 of the British North America Act" (1940) 18 Can. Bar Rev. 517; and see also Shumiatcher, "Section 96 of the B.N.A. Act Re-examined" (1949) 27 Can. Bar Rev. 131.

[12] See, for example, *A. E. Dupont* v. *Inglis* [1958] S.C.R. 535; *Brooks* v. *Pavlick* [1964] S.C.R. 108.

[13] *R.* v. *Hume*; *Consolidated Distilleries Ltd.* v. *Consolidated Exporters Corp. Ltd.* [1930] S.C.R. 531.

wards could only be dealt with by federal legislation under the distribution of legislative power effected by the Constitution.

This provision for federal courts is quite unlike that which undergirds the federal court system in the United States, and is more like the Australian provision, not widely used, which contemplates federal courts to exercise jurisdiction in federal matters although it also goes beyond that.[14] At all events, there is no such thing in Canada as the federal diversity of citizenship jurisdiction that obtains in the United States, or that exists, strangely enough, in the High Court of Australia as an aspect of its original jurisdiction. The power to create federal courts limited to the administration of federal law has not been extensively exercised by Parliament. The Exchequer Court of Canada is the prime example of the resort to that power; and, as its historic name implies it is concerned mainly with the rights and liabilities of the federal Crown, but it also has jurisdiction in patent, copyright and trade mark matters and as an intermediate appellate tribunal in federal tax matters.[15]

There has been no great need in Canada to establish a separate system of federal courts for federal law, because, as a mere matter of course, provincial courts have from the beginning of the Canadian federation exercised jurisdiction in disputes arising out of or involving federal law. Unlike the case in Australia, where the Constitution empowers the Commonwealth Parliament to invest the State courts with jurisdiction in federal matters, the British North America Act is not express on the matter. Inferentially, the legislative

14 See Cowen, *Federal Jurisdiction in Australia* (1960), Chap. 3.
15 Exchequer Court Act, R.S.C. 1952, c. 98, as amended.

authority of the Provinces in relation to the administration of justice therein, and including the constitution, organisation and maintenance of provincial courts both of civil and criminal jurisdiction—without limitation as to matters within federal competence—is an indication of the availability of provincial courts for litigating federal causes of action and for enforcing federal criminal law.[16] The Canadian practice in this respect must depend too on the right of Parliament to impose duties upon provincial courts and upon provincially appointed judicial officers. This right has the highest judicial confirmation [17]; and it follows that provincial courts may be expressly endowed with federal jurisdiction if they do not already possess it as a matter of the continuation of their pre-1867 authority. They may be considered, *pro tanto*, as federal courts in so far as they administer federal law.

The case law on the subject has in recent years gone as far as to support provincial legislative power to vest its courts with jurisdiction in federal matters if there is no federal legislation to the contrary.[18] This view of the omnicompetence of provincial superior courts was fed by a decision of the Privy Council, suggestive of inherent superior court jurisdiction, that (to use its words) " if the right exists, the presumption is that there is a Court which can enforce it, for if no other mode of enforcing it is prescribed, that alone is sufficient to give jurisdiction to the [Queen's] Courts of justice." [19]

The use of provincial courts to administer federal law has given rise to some questions about the procedure to be

[16] British North America Act, s. 92 (14).

[17] *Re Vancini* (1904) 34 S.C.R. 621; *Coughlin* v. *Ontario Highway Transport Board* [1968] S.C.R. 569.

[18] See *Att.-Gen. B.C.* v. *McKenzie* [1965] S.C.R. 490.

[19] *Board* v. *Board* [1919] A.C. 956 at p. 962.

followed in those courts when dealing with causes of action turning on federal legislation. It is sensible enough to say that a litigant seeking to enforce a federal cause of action must take the procedure of the provincial court as he finds it, if Parliament has not seen fit to prescribe its own procedure, which it can do [20]; an example of the latter is in the bankruptcy rules through which jurisdiction in bankruptcy and insolvency is exercised by provincial courts under federal legislation. There have been situations, however, where provincial legislation, alleged to be procedural, has been attacked as unconstitutional as dealing with substantive law in a matter falling within federal power alone. The Province can regulate the procedure of its courts, subject to supersession by federal legislation on the processing of litigation in federal matters; but the Province cannot invade federal legislative authority.[21] What emerges is a special instance of the " substance versus procedure " issue which is familiar in the conflict of laws.

A conspicuous gap in the definition of judicial power under the Canadian Constitution is the want of any provision for jurisdiction in controversies between the Provinces or between the Dominion and a Province. Since this is covered in the earlier American Constitution and in the later Australian one, the Canadian omission might be counted as a reflex of unitary state thinking. No Province can compel another to submit to a particular forum, and certainly a Province cannot compel submission of the federal Crown to judicial process. Nor is it altogether clear whether Parlia-

[20] See *Att.-Gen. Alta. and Winstanley* v. *Atlas Lumber Co.* [1941] S.C.R. 87 at p. 100.

[21] *Reference re Debt Adjustment Act* [1942] S.C.R. 31, affirmed [1943] A.C. 356.

ment (which, as is indicated below, may within limits bind the provincial Crown) can make a Province answerable in a court as a defendant without its consent. Jurisdiction by consent is provided for under the federal Exchequer Court Act which must be supplemented for that purpose by complementary provincial legislation. Even if this be an operative scheme—and there is very little evidence that it is—there is the important question of the determination of the applicable law.

With no jurisdictional foundation upon which to build experience, there can only be an appeal to principle and to such dicta as have been uttered on the question. If jurisdiction is consensual, it might be expected that the consenting parties would at the same time prescribe the legal frame of reference for the issues that are to be adjudicated. Absent such prescription, the court would be left to its own choice of law from available doctrines applicable in similar disputes between citizens, but with adaptations as may be necessary in view of the character of the parties.[22] The assumption in all this is, to use a difficult term, that the dispute is justiciable. Experience in the United States with boundary disputes between states and with disputes on water rights, and experience in Australia of suits between states or between Commonwealth and states, provide guidance in this respect. The Supreme Court of Canada, in hearing an appeal in an issue between Canada and Ontario, originally submitted by consent to the Exchequer Court, stated that since the controversy was about rights, the presupposition was that there was a rule or principle of law upon which those rights

[22] See the discussion of this matter in *Dominion of Canada* v. *Province of Ontario* (1909) 42 S.C.R. 1 at p. 118, affirmed [1910] A.C. 637.

should be determined. The Privy Council took the same view on an appeal in this very case, saying that "in order to succeed the appellants must bring their claim within some recognized legal principle." [23]

Obviously the applicable principle could not rest on the exercise of the legislative power of either of two disputing Provinces, or on that of the Dominion or of a Province where the dispute is between them. A court seized of such a dispute would not be likely to find the law of the case in legislation enacted by one of the litigants to its own advantage.[24]

The Crown in Canada

British constitutional theory, especially in the heyday of Empire, could envisage the indivisibility of the Crown without making a sharp distinction between the Monarch personally and as the legal executive, and, certainly, without fracturing the singleness of the executive authority exercisable from Whitehall. Beyond this, the Crown was also the personification of the state, endowed with capacity to own and dispose of property, to assert rights and accept liabilities but yet entitled as sovereign to certain privileges and immunities in its relations with its citizens.

Canadian federalism did not initially shake this executive unity when in law and in fact Her (indivisible) Majesty was the authority through which a colony was obliged to enter into an international agreement; and when, moreover, a treaty or international agreement between Her Majesty and

23 [1910] A.C. 637 at p. 645. *Cf.* also *Att.-Gen. Quebec* v. *Att.-Gen. Ontario* [1910] A.C. 627, affirming 42 S.C.R. 161.

24 I exclude, of course, those situations in which federal legislation may competently embrace the Province.

a foreign state could be made binding in all British colonies or Dominions as well as in Great Britain. After it was determined by the Privy Council that the Queen was the executive head of the provincial governments no less than of the central government,[25] although represented by and counselled by different persons and advisers at the respective levels, the maintenance of the concept of the indivisibility of the Crown within Canada required a sophistry which was reflected, for example, in emphasis on Her Majesty personally as being vested with title to property, whether it was that of Canada or of a Province, but acknowledging that different administering persons or bodies would wield effective control.[26] This simply confused the Crown as executive and the Crown as personification of the state, but contributed nothing to its evident differentiation as federal and provincial executive. It was a lingering grasp of unreality which no longer has any international legal significance since Canada can contract with foreign states independently and in a name or style other than through Her Majesty if it so pleases.

Nor should anyone be misled as to internal situations within Canada, whether Canada and a Province are involved or two or more Provinces. Her Majesty has no personal physical presence in Canada—if it were ever necessary to consider some question of personal immunity in respect of Canadian law it would be simple enough to recognise it as a common law or even a constitutional principle—and only the legal connotation, the abstraction that Her Majesty or the Crown represents, need be considered for purposes of

[25] *Liquidators of the Maritime Bank* v. *Receiver-General of New Brunswick* [1892] A.C. 437.

[26] See *St. Catherine's Milling and Lumber Co.* v. *R.* (1889) 14 App.Cas. 46 at p. 56; *Re Silver Bros. Ltd.* [1932] A.C. 514 at p. 524.

Canadian federalism. The fact that Interpretation Acts, whether the federal Act or provincial Acts, give the term "Her Majesty" or the "Crown" a personal meaning, is anachronism [27]; it is Canada that is the fictional person, or Ontario or some other Province, as the case may be, where the Crown in one or other of its Canadian aspects personifies the state. Even the British North America Act, as in its property provisions, found it more realistic to speak of property of Canada or property of the Provinces rather than to speak of property vested in Her Majesty.[28]

Where it is necessary to personify the state, whether it be Canada or a Province, the common reference to the Crown has been modified by the addition of an identifying phrase "in right of Canada" or in right of the particular Province. This is recognition that it makes no sense juristically to insist that it is the same Crown that is meant when in fact it is not Her Majesty who is involved.

The three roles that the Crown plays—as a branch of the legislature, as the executive authority and as the personification of the State—require differentiation for purposes of Canadian federalism although this may have been unnecessary in unitary Great Britain. The British North America Act dealt to a degree with the Crown's role as a branch of the legislature, in respect of both Dominion and Provinces—for example, the role of its representatives in assenting to or refusing to assent to or reserving Bills [29]—and it dealt also but quite generally with its executive authority at the federal and provincial level.[30] What the Constitution

[27] Interpretation Act, 1967–68 (Can.), c. 7, s. 28 (15); Interpretation Act, R.S.O. 1960, c. 191, s. 30 (9).

[28] See ss. 107–110, 117.

[29] See ss. 55, 56, 57 and 90.

[30] See ss. 9, 12, 64 and 65.

did not do was to deal with the Crown as the State, whether Canada or the Provinces, not even with respect to judicial power over inter-governmental disputes; and apart from a provision declaring the constitutional immunity from taxation of the property of Canada or of a Province,[31] there is nothing that bears on the so-called prerogatives, the immunities and privileges, attaching to the Crown in its aspect as the State.

The law and learning of Crown privileges and immunities came to the colonies as received or imposed English law, and through section 129 of the British North America Act they were absorbed into the Canadian federation. So far as executive authority was concerned, a distribution had to be effected as between Dominion and Provinces, because unless executive powers were given a constitutional immunity from limitation or extinction, they would remain subordinate to the supremacy of legislation, and hence to that legislature having legislative competence in the particular matter. The adaptation of this English principle to federalism was not difficult; the courts declared that the distribution of executive authority followed the distribution of legislative authority.[32] The one exception that has emerged is in respect of treaty-making and treaty-implementing power; there is plenary federal executive power to enter into international agreements on any matter—there is no court holding to the contrary—but, as is well known, it has been decided at the highest judicial level that the federal legislative power of implementation of such agreements (where negotiated by Canada independently) extends only to such of them as involve

[31] s. 125.
[32] *Bonanza Creek Gold Mining Co. Ltd.* v. *R.* [1916] 1 A.C. 566 at p. 579.

matters that are otherwise within federal legislative competence.[33] This is a constitutional anomaly which has no basis in the text of the British North America Act, and has been criticised even by a member of the Privy Council who was (so far as the formal record goes—the Privy Council then gave only one opinion) a party to the decision.[34] The recent and not entirely quieted debate in Canada on the power of the Provinces to make international agreements was, of course, fed by the anomaly. Short of a constitutional amendment, the Supreme Court will eventually have to face up to the question whether the federal executive power in treaty-making is too broad or its legislative power of implementation is too narrow.

The most difficult problems raised by the bifurcated position of the Crown in Canadian federalism arise out of its role as being in a juristic sense the State, that is, Canada or a Province. Its role as a branch of the federal legislature and of the provincial legislatures is protected against any legislation of the other, and even as against adverse legislation of the very legislature of which it is a branch; this is fundamental law.[35] Again, its provincial executive role is not, in respect of its discharge of provincial governmental responsibilities, subject to any derogating federal legislation or derogating federal executive power and is affected only by the provisions in the British North America Act for reservation and disallowance of provincial Bills and legislation respectively,

33 *Att.-Gen. Can.* v. *Att.-Gen. Ont.* [1937] A.C. 326.

34 Lord Wright in (1955) 33 Can. Bar Rev. 1123 at p. 1127; see also Rand, "Some Aspects of Canadian Constitutionalism" (1960) 38 Can. Bar Rev. 135 at p. 142.

35 Emphasised by British North America Act, s. 92 (1), empowering the provincial legislature to amend the Constitution of the Province, except as regards the office of Lieutenant-Governor; see *Re Initiative and*

provisions which are dormant if not entirely dead.[36] What then of the interaction of federal and provincial legislative power and legislation where the Crown provincial and the Crown federal act as juristic persons, contracting with citizens or even with each other, holding property, or suing or being sued in respect of claims cognizable under the common law or under legislation?

Just as Canada may contract internationally, with Great Britain or with Australia for example, it may equally contract with a Province, and so also may two Provinces contract; and it is mere word-playing or play-acting to say that because a person cannot at common law contract with himself, there cannot in law be a contract to which Her Majesty is a party on each side.[37] Nor does the question of enforceability in a judicial forum give rise to difficulty. If a subject can sue the Crown in contract in a proper forum, the same privilege may be exercised where the contract is between Province and Dominion, albeit formally styled as between Her Majesty in right of the Province and Her Majesty in right of Canada, or as between two Provinces, correspondingly styled. The federal Crown is suable in the Exchequer Court; the provincial Crown in the superior court of the particular Province; either may sue in the other forum because the Crown (or the state) is a competent plaintiff.

At common law it was not in all respects, certainly not in tort, suable as a defendant. Alleviation of this immunity

Referendum Act [1919] A.C. 935; and see also ss. 55, 90 and 91 (1) (enacted by 1949 (U.K.), c. 81).

36 See LaForest, *Disallowance and Reservation of Provincial Legislation* (1955) for the history of these matters.

37 *Cf. Reference re Troops in Cape Breton* [1930] S.C.R. 554. Proper authority would, of course, have to be established; certainly, if federal or provincial revenues were to be committed.

in favour of the subject required, of course, separate federal and provincial legislation. This immunity, as other advantages enjoyed by the Crown as a juristic person and litigant, developed outside of any framework of federalism; but as they arose for decision in Canada they had somehow to be fitted into the distributive scheme. The unitary position was comparatively simple; a question of construction alone was involved where legislation allegedly diminished or extinguished Her Majesty's common law immunities or privileges. Similarly, the question was constructional only in the relation of federal legislation to the federal Crown and of provincial legislation to the Crown in right of the Province.[38] In this respect, there was another application of the principle that the distribution of legislative power carries the correlative distribution of prerogative power. The question remained, however, how far the generality of the Crown's privileges and immunities, for example, the right to priority of payment as a creditor or immunity from tort liability, could be asserted in the right of a Province against federal legislation or in the right of Canada against provincial legislation, and how far advantage could be taken of such legislation in each case.

Judicial decision has established that federal legislation, competently enacted of course, may embrace the Crown in right of a Province and may even expropriate provincial Crown property.[39] Federal legislation, in brief, may deal with the provincial Crown as if it were an ordinary subject, liable to be bound by the federal Parliament, and may also

[38] For an illustration, see *Canadian Broadcasting Corp.* v. *Att.-Gen. Ontario* [1959] S.C.R. 188.

[39] *R.* v. *Board of Transport Commissioners* (1968) 65 D.L.R. (2d) 421; *Att.-Gen. Quebec* v. *Nipissing Central Ry.* [1926] A.C. 715.

deal with its privileges and immunities in so far as they may relate to matters that fall within federal legislative power. For example, since bankruptcy and insolvency are within the catalogue of exclusive federal powers, Parliament may subordinate a claim of the provincial Crown to priority of payment of a claim against a bankrupt's estate. If there has been no express or necessarily intended subordination, the prerogative in question may be asserted on the basis of the principle, which has been given federal standing so to speak, that the Crown's prerogatives cannot be affected unless this is done expressly or by necessary intendment; no distinction is made as between federal and provincial Crown in recognition of such prerogatives where not competently limited or destroyed.[40]

Correlative competence of provincial legislation to embrace the federal Crown has not, however, been recognised. The theory of denial of such reach to provincial enactments may be that the federal Crown is external both to the provincial catalogue of powers as well as to the territorial ambit of provincial legislation; territoriality is a limiting factor in the exercise of provincial legislative power, but no longer (if it ever was) in the exercise of federal legislative power.[41] Nor is logic a constitutional imperative calling for reciprocal authority.

On similar reasoning a provincial legislature would be incompetent to bind the Crown in right of another Province. It is not so much a question of the relation of foreign states as it is of the scope of legislative power; it has been held, for example, and wisely I think, that a Province is not a

40 *R.* v. *Breton* [1967] S.C.R. 503; *Re Silver Bros. Ltd.* [1932] A.C. 514.

41 Statute of Westminster 1931 (U.K.), s. 3; and see *Croft* v. *Dunphy* [1933] A.C. 156.

foreign country *vis-à-vis* another Province in respect of the enforcement in the latter of the former's revenue laws.[42] Canada is under no such legislative disability, of course, and there is no reason why the " revenue laws " principle should apply as between units of the same federation.

The immunity of the federal Crown from provincial legislation—the Supreme Court of Canada put it rather starkly in a recent case in saying that " the Crown in the right of Canada cannot be bound by a provincial statute " [43]—must be set against what I regard as a curious contradiction of this principle in the subjection of the federal Crown to pre-1867 provincial law which was carried into post-1867 Canada as part of that law. Thus, it has been held that the federal Crown could not assert priority against other unsecured creditors in respect of a claim against a bank in liquidation, nor (in a judgment given, strangely, against the federal Crown on its consent to reversal of a judgment below in its favour) was it entitled to priority in a claim against the estate of a deceased debtor, where the law in force before 1867 and which was carried forward in each case denied priority to the Crown.[44] Of course, there was no federal Crown before 1867, but, apart from this, it seems incongruous to apply surviving pre-1867 provincial law to defeat the federal Crown when the Province could not have enacted such legislation against the federal Crown after confederation.

It remains to mention the position of the federal Crown

[42] *Weir* v. *Lohr* (1967) 65 D.L.R. (2d) 717. The orthodox doctrine was affirmed by the Supreme Court of Canada in *U.S.A.* v. *Harden* [1963] S.C.R. 366.

[43] *R.* v. *Breton* [1967] S.C.R. 503 at p. 506.

[44] *Exchange Bank* v. *R.* (1886) 11 App.Cas. 157; *Re Mendelsohn* (1960) 25 D.L.R. (2d) 778, reversing by consent 22 D.L.R. (2d) 748.

(or, indeed, the Crown in right of another Province) where it sues in a provincial forum and must or seeks to rely on the legislation of the Province to realise its claim. Here, where there is no question of defeating or denying a federal Crown prerogative existing, of course, apart from the legislation, it seems entirely proper that the federal Crown should take the legislation as a whole—with its burdens as well as its benefits. Thus, if as a master it sues in a *per quod* action to recover loss by reason of injury suffered by a servant through another's negligence, it must accept the provincial law governing the liability of the negligent person including apportionment legislation.[45]

THE LAW IN THE FEDERAL COURTS: FEDERAL LAW IN THE PROVINCIAL COURTS

Two propositions, already stated, must be repeated to give context to what follows in this section. First, in Canada federal legislation is enforceable as of course in provincial superior courts unless this is precluded by federal statute or, unless (and this is hardly likely) the provincial superior court's jurisdiction is not broad enough to encompass it. Second, federal courts of original jurisdiction (or of intermediate appellate jurisdiction, and hence excluding the Supreme Court of Canada) can deal only with causes of action involving federal matters (which include federal Crown liability). Moreover, being statutory courts without the ancestral advantages of the provincial superior courts, it may be said of the federal courts that they have no jurisdiction except such as is expressly conferred, while the

[45] See *R.* v. *Murray* [1967] S.C.R. 262.

provincial superior courts have a comprehensive jurisdiction unless expressly curtailed.

This state of affairs has induced a state of mind which tends to regard all legal issues that fall to be determined on common law principles (rather than under federal legislation) as provincial matters; indeed, the common law tends to be looked upon as provincial, particularly when it might be differently expressed by different provincial courts, although it is recognised that it may be in a field in which federal legislation would be competent. Moreover, since, for example, the principles of liability in negligence are applicable, absent any valid limiting legislation, to the widest variety of situations and relationships (some of which might be matters for provincial legislation and some for federal), their uniform application emphasises the provincial character of the law in all those situations and relationships. The same thing would be true in respect of the law of contracts, the law of agency and so on.

This is inevitable, and is, in any event, the preferable course in litigation in the provincial courts; they should not be expected to fashion a separate rule of tort liability or of liability in contract for an activity or relationship which could be brought under federal regulation (but has not been), differing from the rule applied to activities or relationships subject to provincial legislative regulation, unless there is something in the character of those matters which calls for a different measure. However, this attitude has been carried over into litigation in the federal Exchequer Court, and has extended to the application therein of general provincial legislation as well as the common law, although that court is, by constitutional directive, limited to the enforcement of federal law only.

This has come about, or can be explained, on one or other of two grounds, if not on both. First, provincial law may be applicable on a theory of referential incorporation or adoption, either expressly or by necessary implication. This is the case with the federal Crown Liability Act which makes the federal Crown liable, as if it were a private person, vicariously for the tort of a servant and also in respect of a breach of duty attaching to the ownership, occupation, possession or control of property.[46] It is the law of the Province where the tort occurs that governs the liability, a point emphasised by the definition of " tort " in the Act to mean delict or quasi-delict in respect of any matter arising in Quebec. This is not expressed in the statute but is taken to be implicit. Second, where no rules of law for determining liability are stated in a federal statute enforceable in a federal court, and even if the federal Crown is a litigant, it is the general law between subject and subject that applies; and this again brings in the particular provincial law, subject, however, to a caveat on its application if it would impose a liability on the federal Crown or, as the Supreme Court has said, derogate from " existing Crown prerogatives, privileges or rights." [47]

The consequence of this view is seen in the *per quod* cases brought by the federal Crown to recover for loss of services of an employee injured by another person's negligence. Where the injury has occurred in a common law Province the Crown has succeeded in this type of suit, provided the injured servant could himself have sued the tortfeasor. But where the claim arose as a result of injury in Quebec,

[46] See Crown Liability Act, 1952–53 (Can.), c. 30.
[47] *R.* v. *Murray* [1967] S.C.R. 262 at p. 268.

the Crown has failed because an action *per quod* in the broad terms known to the common law was unknown to the civil law and had to be brought within the delictual provisions of the Civil Code.[48]

The obvious question that arises is why does not the federal court fashion its own rules of law in the federal matters committed to its jurisdiction. If it is not expressly enjoined to apply provincial law—and that application, as is evident, may bring different results in the same situation—would it not be appropriate to consider a truly federal "common law," along the lines that are developing in the United States, similarly in federal matters there, after the decision of its Supreme Court in *Erie Railroad Co.* v. *Tompkins*? [49] To take one possibility, the federal court might well bring the law of occupiers' liability into better concordance with the general principles of negligence than is now the case under the provincial elaborations; it is not necessary to wait for an Occupiers' Liability Act to do the job.

The only constitutional toe-hold for such an exercise of judicial power is, as has already been indicated, that portion of section 101 of the British North America Act which empowers Parliament to establish additional courts "for the better administration of the laws of Canada." Reliance on this and on the paramountcy doctrine of the Constitution in favour of the primacy of federal legislation would support the inclusion of judge-made law under the words of section 101; similar contentions on similar grounds have been made to justify the evolution of a federal common law in the United

[48] Contrast *Att.-Gen. Canada* v. *Jackson* [1946] S.C.R. 489 and *R.* v. *Sylvain* [1965] S.C.R. 164.

[49] (1938) 304 U.S. 64.

States within the same limits of national legislative jurisdiction.[50] There appears, however, to be no case in which the possibility of such a federal common law in Canada has been explored.[51] However, there is as much warrant for such an approach as there is for the "provincial law" approach which has been adopted without even as strong a constitutional base.[52]

No doubt, one of the reasons for the now almost casual assumption of the application of provincial law is the fact that, without express federal legislative sanction, provincial courts have been making the law on what for convenience may be termed federal causes of action. But there are others as well. The Supreme Court of Canada is a unifying court, at least for the common law Provinces, in a sense that the Supreme Court of the United States is not; and, further, it can and does declare the law of the Province in provincial causes of action which, again, the Supreme Court of the United States cannot do in respect of state law.[53] Moreover, the particular position of Quebec, with its Civil Code and its Code of Procedure, suggests an accommodation to its legal system which Parliament and not the courts should deign to remove. It may be said, of course, that there are areas of the law within federal legislative power, for example, in the field of admiralty, where neither the common law nor the

[50] See Note, "The Federal Common Law" (1969) 82 Harv.L.Rev. 1512.

[51] To the contrary, in a recent case on the Admiralty side of the Exchequer Court of Canada it was held that the Quebec law applied because the matter arose there; see *Barthe* v. *LeNavire S/S Florida* [1969] 1 Ex.C.R. 299.

[52] Is not the result of this approach that the provincial courts (subject to the direction of the Supreme Court of Canada) have a law-making power that the provincial legislatures do not have?

[53] See, generally, Willis, "Securing Uniformity of Law in a Federal System—Canada" (1944) 5 U.T.L.J. 352.

Quebec civil law can claim any standing; and if judge-made law exists here as a body of federal doctrine why should there be a reluctance to expand the initiative of the federal courts? The answer must be a pragmatic one, without attempting to throw over it the superficial cloak that Parliament can always establish the particular norms of obligation or liability; Parliament will not, save in special cases, do this because it is essentially a job for the courts.

No doubt a federal court like the Exchequer Court of Canada in applying provincial law may be mistaken in what that law is; but there is the corrective jurisdiction of the Supreme Court of Canada in such a situation, as there is where a provincial court's exposition of the law of the Province is challenged. The Exchequer Court is not necessarily bound to accept the statement of what is the provincial law from the course of decision of the highest court of the Province; it may choose to determine it for itself, resting on the knowledge that the Supreme Court of Canada is back of it as it is back of the provincial appellate courts. The curious result of all this is that just as the provincial courts are expositors of federal law, so are the federal courts expositors of provincial law.

The difference between the two sets of courts in the source of their organisation and in their jurisdiction does not alone bring into view another difference, constitutionally decreed, namely, the language of pleading and process and of advocacy. Section 133 of the British North America Act makes English and French permissible languages in the Quebec courts and in the federal courts (as well as in the legislative chambers of Quebec and of Canada). This provision has a history in usage and in law which has been fully canvassed in Book I of the *Report of the Royal Commission on Bilingualism and*

Biculturalism published in late 1967. Although similar provision was made for the permitted use of English or French in the courts of Manitoba (as well as in legislative debate) when it was admitted to Confederation in 1870, and so too in the courts and council debates in the Northwest Territories in 1877, these enactments were later repealed (that respecting Manitoba not without some doubt as to the constitutionality of the repealing statute), and English was substituted as the official language. None of the other Provinces are constitutionally affected by either section 133 or any comparable measure; it is for them to determine the language of their courts and of their legislative chambers and of other governmental operations.

It will be recalled that British legislation of 1731 provided that after March 25, 1733, all proceedings in any court of justice in England should be in the English tongue and language only "and not in Latin or French or any other tongue or language whatsoever." Recently in British Columbia, a French speaking accused claimed the right to trial in French, contending that the provincial magistrate's court before which he was appearing was, in respect of the enforcement of the federal Criminal Code, a federal court, and hence section 133 of the British North America Act applied. The British Columbia courts rejected the contention, holding that the British statute was included in the English law received in the Province and that the magistrate's court was not a "Court of Canada established under the [British North America] Act," to quote the relevant words of section 133.[54] The distinction between a federally established court

[54] *R.* v. *Watts, ex p. Poulin* (1968) 69 D.L.R. (2d) 526, affirmed (1968) 1 D.L.R. (3d) 239.

and a provincial court exercising federal jurisdiction was open on the wording of section 133 but the consequence of the distinction has been blunted by the new Official Languages Act of 1969, which carries out recommendations made by the Royal Commission on Bilingualism and Biculturalism in its Report previously mentioned.

This federal enactment, besides declaring the official character and the equality in status, and in rights and privileges as to their use, of English and French for all the purposes of and in all the institutions of the Parliament and Government of Canada, goes on to deal with specific situations in which the use of the two languages is either mandatory or open. Among the latter is the vesting of discretion in provincial courts exercising federal criminal jurisdiction to order, at the request of the accused and if it appears to the court that this can effectively be done, that the proceedings be conducted wholly or mainly in one of the official languages. However, the implementation of this provision is postponed until a discretion in the provincial courts or in their judges as to the language of proceedings in civil causes or matters is provided for by provincial law. The constitutional base for this particular provision is, of course, in section 91 (27) of the British North America Act which gives Parliament exclusive legislative authority in relation to the criminal law and to procedure in criminal matters.

INDEX

PRINTED IN GREAT BRITAIN
BY
THE EASTERN PRESS LTD.
OF LONDON AND READING